LIVING WITH GRIEF

Living with Grief provides a guide to how to live when others have died.

Written by a therapist and counsellor who specialises in Grief, Loss and Bereavement, it helps readers gain insight into some of the processes that might be happening when things feel overwhelming. Following an effective Q&A framework, it offers a valuable 'dip in and out' approach with good signposting to guidance on all the questions that those touched by grief need to know. Organised into short manageable chapters, the book provides strategies to offer understanding and compassion to gently encourage readers to think about what is going on for them during this time. It introduces a diverse and inclusive cast of characters who are going through grief themselves in various different circumstances to reflect modern culture and the issues people face. It also includes coverage about the social context in which the griever lives and the role of social media and how that can play into competitive and performative aspects of grief.

This book acts as a compassionate companion for those figuring out how to live with grief. It is also valuable reading for counsellors, mental health professionals and other health and social care professionals.

Sara Mathews is a qualified Counselling Supervisor and Trainer with over 12,500 hours of clinical experience. She is Accredited and Registered with the British Association of Counselling and Psychotherapy (BACP) and a certified Online and Telephone

Counsellor. She headed up bereavement services in the voluntary sector for many years before setting up her own counselling practice. She is passionate about working in a properly trauma-informed way with her clients, and also offers supervision or consultation to therapists, health care and allied professionals.

BPS ASK THE EXPERTS IN PSYCHOLOGY SERIES

Routledge, in partnership with the British Psychological Society (BPS), is pleased to present BPS Ask the Experts, a new popular science series that addresses key issues and answers the burning questions. Drawing on the expertise of established psychologists, every book in the series provides authoritative and straightforward guidance on pressing topics that matter to real people in their everyday lives.

All books in the BPS Ask the Experts series are written for the reader with no prior knowledge or experience. For answers to everything you ever wanted to know about issues important to you, ask the expert!

Understanding and Helping to Overcome Exam Anxiety
What Is It, Why Is It Important and Where Does It Come from?
David W. Putwain

Understanding Artificial Minds through Human Minds
The Psychology of Artificial Intelligence
Max M. Louwerse

Rising to the Challenge of Life after Cancer
Expert Advice for Finding Wellness
Jeffrey Charles Dunn and Suzanne Kathleen Chambers

Building a Psychologically Safe Work Environment
Binna Kandola

Understanding Climate Anxiety
Geoffrey Beattie

Living Well with Parkinson's
A Guide to a Fulfilling Life
Angeliki Bogosian

Living with Grief
A Compassionate Companion
Sara Mathews

For more information about this series, please visit: https://www.routledge.com/BPS-Ask-The-Experts-in-Psychology-Series/book-series/BPSATE.

LIVING WITH GRIEF

A COMPASSIONATE COMPANION

SARA MATHEWS

LONDON AND NEW YORK

Designed cover image: Westend61/Getty Images

First published 2026
by Routledge
4 Park Square, Milton Park, Abingdon, Oxon OX14 4RN

and by Routledge
605 Third Avenue, New York, NY 10158

Routledge is an imprint of the Taylor & Francis Group, an informa business

© 2026 Sara Mathews

The right of Sara Mathews to be identified as author of this work has been asserted in accordance with sections 77 and 78 of the Copyright, Designs and Patents Act 1988.

All rights reserved. No part of this book may be reprinted or reproduced or utilised in any form or by any electronic, mechanical, or other means, now known or hereafter invented, including photocopying and recording, or in any information storage or retrieval system, without permission in writing from the publishers.

Trademark notice: Product or corporate names may be trademarks or registered trademarks, and are used only for identification and explanation without intent to infringe.

British Library Cataloguing-in-Publication Data
A catalogue record for this book is available from the British Library

Library of Congress Cataloging-in-Publication Data
Names: Mathews, Sara (Counselor) author
Title: Living with grief : a compassionate companion / Sara Mathews.
Description: Abingdon, Oxon ; New York, NY : Routledge, 2026. | Series: BPS ask the experts series | Includes bibliographical references and index.
Identifiers: LCCN 2025030244 (print) | LCCN 2025030245 (ebook) | ISBN 9781032933290 hardback | ISBN 9781032933245 paperback | ISBN 9781003565406 ebook
Subjects: LCSH: Grief | Bereavement | Loss (Psychology)
Classification: LCC BF575.G7 M386 2026 (print) | LCC BF575.G7 (ebook)
LC record available at https://lccn.loc.gov/2025030244
LC ebook record available at https://lccn.loc.gov/2025030245

ISBN: 978-1-032-93329-0 (hbk)
ISBN: 978-1-032-93324-5 (pbk)
ISBN: 978-1-003-56540-6 (ebk)

DOI: 10.4324/9781003565406

Typeset in Joanna MT Std
by codeMantra

CONTENTS

Foreword: Who Am I and Why Am I Giving You This Advice?   viii

   Introduction   1

1 Will It Always Be Like This?   5

2 No More Casseroles – What Happens Next?   25

3 What Is the Dark Side of Grief?   47

4 'You're Not on Your Own' – How to Deal with Other People   71

5 My Grief Feels Different to Other People's – What Should I Do?   93

6 What's the Meaning of Life Now?   115

FOREWORD: WHO AM I AND WHY AM I GIVING YOU THIS ADVICE?

Hello, my name is Sara Mathews and I am a qualified and very experienced therapist with a special interest in working with the bereaved. I trained as a therapist in my forties and qualified in 2009. I have a B.A. honours degree in Counselling and a Certificate in Clinical Supervision, and am accredited with the British Association of Counselling and Psychotherapy. My first professional job was working with clients struggling with addiction and problem gambling. It soon became evident to me that underlying these behavioural challenges there was often a lot of unresolved grief resulting from bereavement. An interest was sparked for me that has increased over many years and many thousands of hours of clinical practice. I moved from that first job into the hospice sector where I worked for 12 years delivering and, in the end, managing bereavement counselling services for clients both young and old, and everything else in between.

All the while I was reading and going on training courses and learning as much as I could about grief, loss, death, dying and bereavement. Valuable though all of that was – and still is because there is always another book to read including mine now, and another dimension to living with grief to think about – nothing taught me as much as the hours and hours spent in the company of clients. Listening to those people tell their stories and trying to support them as they struggled to find ways to live with grief is what has given me the confidence and the drive to want to write this book. I have endeavoured to recreate some fictitious characters who I hope will help you to learn things that might prove useful to you as you try to figure out how to live with your grief. My characters are fictional but the many relationships I have had with real people dealing with real loss, are what they are based on. There's no substitute for experience in my view.

Which leads me to the more personal aspects of my own life and the losses I have struggled with that have driven me to want to explore the human experience of grief and try to offer something useful to those who are struggling too. I'm not unique; it's probably true to say that at some point we will all be touched by death and loss and feel the unmistakable devastation of grief. Over the last 20 years both my parents have died. I have lost two friends, one of whom tragically took her own life, and a number of much-loved cats to whom I was devoted. All those losses matter to me in different ways and have affected me differently.

Grief, as I say in the first paragraph of my book, is universal and yet we shy away from it. We often avoid talking about it or even acknowledging that it's not if we die but when. It's coming for us all. So why not try to find compassionate, informed and sensible ways to live with the feelings that death engenders, specifically grief. It's not a specialist subject really, or at least it shouldn't be. My mission is not to set myself up as an unattainable and intimidating expert but instead to offer a way of thinking about grief that will help you to realise that awful though it is, we can find ways to live with it.

I'm in my sixties now and still working as a therapist in private practice. I spend my working days connecting with people through the miracle of technology (some people call it Zoom; other platforms are of course available!) I am still learning and I am still amazed at the courage and endurance we can find within ourselves to live with pain and grief. It is my belief that we can learn from each other to make that most human of tasks a bit easier and it is that belief that has driven me to want to share my learning and offer you some support. I hope it helps.

INTRODUCTION

I believe that most of us are living with grief of one sort or another. To me grief, sorrow and loss are inescapable parts of what it is to be human and therefore to care about people, animals, aspects of self and the world in which we live. Whenever anything changes there is the potential to feel the loss of what is no more. So we begin with the idea that grief is universal, unavoidable and something we have to learn to live with. The simple act of getting older each day contains within it a certain amount of loss; the loss of youthful optimism, an unlined face, the ability to stay up late and barely notice the difference the following day. However, my guess is that if you are reading this book, it might be because you are dealing with what is often the biggest loss that any of us encounter in our lives and that is of course the death of someone we care about. This book is for you and is based on things I have learned during my career as a grief therapist. I think it will also be useful if you are interested in supporting others, either personally or professionally. Or perhaps you are simply a good human. The kind of person who wants to know about the things that affect us all and live as good a life as you can. It might sound an odd thing to say but during my 17 years as a grief therapist — in which time I have dealt with the death of both of my parents, two close friends and four beloved cats, I have learned that living with grief as best I can has allowed me to live better. I have learned things about myself, about other people, what connects us and what makes us different from each other. I have learned from some truly extraordinary people that it is possible to learn to live with grief and that these are not feelings you have to get over in order to carry on. Quite the contrary: grief can become part of our lives alongside of memories, connections and continuing love if that's what you feel. I hope reading this book helps you to learn some of those same things for yourself.

Whatever your reason for finding your way to these pages you are welcome here and if you are actively grieving for someone right now, then I am truly sorry for your loss. You will already know that there are no magic formulas – although there can be something called magical thinking that we will get to in due course. Perhaps most importantly there are no rules. You can't do grief the wrong way, you can only do it your way. This book will help you gain insight into some of the processes that might be happening for you when things feel overwhelming and you barely recognise yourself. You can pick this book up, read a bit and put it down again. Everything is organised into manageable, short chapters. Grieving people need rest so take your time and try the best you can to attend to what you feel as you read. That is how you will truly learn to live with your grief, from your own responses and needs and the awareness that the only formula is the one that works for you. One of the many strange conundrums of grief is that you need to feel it in order to free it and live with it. It is perfectly natural to want to keep away from that which hurts us. Most of us learn early on in life to only put our hand in the fire once. After that we know how much it hurts and try to avoid burning our fingers again if we can possibly avoid it. Grief, however, requires of us that we stop pulling away and learn instead to tolerate it. We need to allow grief to be felt and crucially, allow it to teach us how we are going to live alongside of it. My aim for this book is that it acts as a compassionate companion for you as you figure how you are going to do that, one small step at a time.

A large amount of what you read here is based on my experience working as a grief therapist. My first job after qualifying as a therapist was working with clients dealing with problem gambling and substance abuse of various kinds. I soon learned that these behaviours were often – but not always – connected to grief and loss and had begun as ways to distract people from other pain before gaining a terrifying momentum of their own. From there I began my work in the hospice sector working with clients who had experienced the death of someone significant. You might even be one of those people reading this book right now as there are quite a lot of you. To date I have completed roughly 13,000 hours of grief therapy. I will not be sharing any of those stories here because client confidentiality is something I take extremely seriously. What I will be sharing is a series of fictitious characters that I have created to help me share some of the lessons of grief. You will meet them in each chapter and through them we can begin to explore some important ideas about grief and what it's like to live alongside of it in real life situations.

Here are some ideas about things you might find helpful to do for yourself as you read this book. The first is to notice how you feel in response to the things you read. Do you agree? Is your experience similar to the ideas and characters that appear on these pages or is it different? This isn't a manual on how to do grief because that would be far too prescriptive and make what I believe to be the wrong-headed assumption that we can generalise about what grief is like. Instead, it is intended to offer a range of ideas and experiences and some prompts for you to consider how it is for you and how you can live with your reality as opposed to someone else's. Once you get used to noticing how you feel, try to give yourself permission to have those feelings. It can really help to name a feeling rather than just feel it. Try 'I notice I am feeling exhausted today', or 'full of rage', or 'disconnected and shut off from the world'. Whatever it is you are feeling, notice it, name it and reassure yourself that it's OK to feel whatever it is as that is part of how grief is for you in that moment.

People have often shared with me their concerns that they are doing grief wrong. Which is why it's so important to understand that this is simply not true. There is no blueprint for the complexity of grief. The last thing you need when trying to cope with what may be some of the hardest feelings you have ever had to deal with in your life, is the nagging idea that you are also getting it wrong. Some of the concerns I have heard are that people worry they are not sad enough. That they are not spending every waking moment in tears and that maybe other people will think they don't care. Conversely – which might give you a clue as to how grief really is different for everyone – people worry that they feel too awful, too overwhelmed and shouldn't they be starting to get back to 'normal' now that a certain amount of time has passed. In both these scenarios (and many, many others, some of which we will explore as we go along) the answer is that this is how it is for you today.

'How is it for me today?' is perhaps the single most useful question to ask yourself as you read this book and live this new version of your life. Your answers can give you some important clues as to how best you can learn to look after yourself based on what you need today.

Let's do a quick check in before we move on. Have you been noticing how you feel as you read this introduction? The key ideas contained here are:

- Grief is universal and part of all our lives
- You don't have to get over anything, or forget about someone in order to learn to live with grief
- There are no rules
- You aren't doing it wrong. You are doing it your way and that's OK
- The key to figuring out how to live with something is to tune into what you are feeling and ask yourself what that tells you about what you need right now, in this moment

1

WILL IT ALWAYS BE LIKE THIS?

- What's the point of looking after me when nothing you do is going to change anything?
- What is happening inside my body and brain?
- What can I expect from early grief?
- Is the idea of stages of grief a help or a hindrance?
- Will it always be like this?
- Is anger part of my grief?
- What's the point of looking at my feelings when it's so painful to do so?
- How do I best care for myself in the early days of loss?

WHAT'S THE POINT OF LOOKING AFTER ME WHEN NOTHING YOU DO IS GOING TO CHANGE ANYTHING?

Before we start exploring whether grief changes or stays the same, I want to ask you how you felt at the end of the Introduction when I invited you to think about what you were feeling and what you needed in that moment. Maybe it was something reasonably manageable like feeling tired and fed up of reading, in which case you might have chosen to put this book down, watch a bit of telly, scroll on your phone or just have a rest doing as little as the demands of your life allowed. But maybe what you noticed yourself feeling and therefore what you thought you needed was unrealistic and out of reach. I am writing this during one of the wettest July's the UK has had in a long time. If what I noticed myself feeling is fed up with the rain (I am, by the way) and therefore what I really needed was to feel the sunshine on my shoulders, then that is simply not within my control to be able to achieve in that moment. Maybe if I'm lucky, I can check the forecast and see if the weather is any better over the next few days. Maybe I can, ambitions and finances permitting, book a holiday somewhere warm. Maybe I can find another way to change my feelings by meeting other needs and distract myself from the weather. The point is not to give up noticing what we feel and trying to attend to our needs when we discover we can't always get what we want, not right now and sometimes not at all.

What if the thing you noticed yourself feeling is the awful, cavernous yearning that can come with the death of someone we care about and wish was still alive. That craving and desire for the physical presence of someone, their smell, the sound of their voice. The way the atmosphere in the room changed simply because they were there with us. What if that's how you felt and they were what you needed? That might have stirred all sorts of feelings in you, including what on earth the point of reading this book might be as nothing is going to bring them back.

Guess what? You're right. Nothing is going to bring them back. Whatever spiritual, existential, philosophical or religious sense you make of death we are all broadly in agreement that it is final and we can't have the life we had before, when they were still alive, back again. Forgive me if that sounds blunt but it is one of the most important, and undoubtedly painful things we need to start to come to terms with if we are going to learn to live with our grief. It is very tricky to adapt to a new reality no matter how welcome or unwelcome that reality might be, if we don't accept that a change has occurred.

The slightly better news is that acceptance of change is a process and so we don't have to do it all in a day. Indeed, that would be impossible. When a very dear friend of mine died I simply couldn't believe she was gone. Even now, years later, I still think of her if I hear some music that I think she might have liked, or something that might have made her laugh. I am no longer at the point where I pick up my phone to message her about something but I still think of her. That offers an important clue to the question posed at the beginning of this chapter 'Will it always be like this?' I am going to be bold here – therapists are notoriously cagey about answering direct questions. Some of us were actually trained to never answer a question with anything other than another question directed back at you: 'Well what do you think?' My experience is that this can sometimes be a powerful way to help a client to clarify their own thoughts but often it's just really irritating. My bold assertion is that grief does change. I base this not only on my own experience but the extraordinary opportunity I have had over the years to witness grief changing for many, many people and to hear what they have to say when they realise things are not the same as they once were in the immediate aftermath of death.

WHAT IS HAPPENING INSIDE MY BODY AND BRAIN?

Let me introduce you to Dalia. Dalia's partner and the father of their two young children, has just died. He was diagnosed with end stage pancreatic cancer. Within three weeks of his diagnosis, he died. For those of you unfamiliar with pancreatic cancer the symptoms can be hard to spot. By the time Dalia's partner Dan realised that something was wrong the cancer had already spread to other parts of his body and his prognosis was short. He was told it might be a matter of weeks or months but not years before he died. Nonetheless for Dan to die within three weeks of his diagnosis gave him and his family no time at all to adapt to this new and catastrophic reality. Dalia is left with Ayesha their little girl who is eight and Aaron their son who is five. She is reeling with shock but she has to keep going because the children need her to look after them. She feels like she is in some horrific parallel reality where nothing makes sense to her. Dalia catches herself staring out the window of their flat onto the street below where people appear to be going about their normal business and she can't quite believe what she is seeing. How can people just carry on as normal when her world has quite literally come crashing down around her? Dalia robotically makes food for the children, gets them dressed, walks them to school and does her best to make sure they are safe and cared for. She rarely cries and sometimes she vaguely wonders if the other parents at the school gate think she is awful for just standing there, blank faced as she waves her kids off or comes to collect them.

WHAT CAN I EXPECT FROM EARLY GRIEF?

I think most of us reading about Dalia and imagining as best we can what it might be like to be her in those early days of her grief, would recognise that she is in shock. We might even cast our minds back to when we ourselves first heard the news of the death of someone significant in our own lives and realise that we also went into our own version of shock. I stood out in my back garden the night I learned of my friend's death, she very sadly died by suicide, and shouted wildly into the darkness 'Why? Why did you do this?' I was shocked and angry and bewildered. Then I went inside because it was really cold and thought about what I was doing at work the next day. It never occurred to me to take time off. She was just a friend and I started going to work in the days when bereavement leave was scaled on some pre-determined scale of closeness. You got more days off the 'closer' the person was deemed to be. I never thought to ask if I could have time off. I pushed the feelings down and just tried to get on with life. Needless to say, I paid dearly for this short sightedness later down the line when I experienced a pretty awful emotional crash. Dalia can't take time off from looking after her children as whilst there are friends and some family about for her, she feels she must be with her children. She needs to be the person who is there for them now that they only have her and even letting them out of her sight so they can go to school is a desperate struggle for her.

Shock, like a lot of things the brain does, is functional. **Colin Murray Parkes**, one of the first writers I came to treasure for his writing on grief, talks about how the brain quickly recognises that something is wrong and swings into action, sometimes referred to as arousal that Parkes described as 'Alarm'. It does this to help us manage threat and keep ourselves and those we care about safe. I can well imagine that Dalia's brain is highly focussed on keeping her children safe in a world that has very suddenly become unpredictable and potentially dangerous. When we are in this state of alarm or arousal, when something shocking has happened that we can barely comprehend, the brain focusses on doing the things it needs to do to keep safe. This might mean that other things it does perfectly well in more stable times take a back seat. One of the things that it might do a bit less of is noticing feelings. Which can account for why people feel cut off from their emotions as if they are floating about in some strange version of a world they no longer recognise.

As with most things in life, thinking around grief is evolving. Some of us will recall generations above us describing not having the time to grieve as they simply had to get on with it. This was my grandmother's somewhat uncompromising view about talking about difficult feelings in general, including grief. I think she thought acknowledging feelings was a dangerous strategy that might result in feeling overwhelmed and worse than before. Better to put up and shut up. This didn't stop her from being terrified of thunderstorms and always feeling the need to get under the kitchen table if she heard thunder. Not that surprising when you consider she lived through World War II and lived in London when it was heavily bombed. Nowadays we would probably describe my grandmother as suffering from Post Traumatic Stress Disorder. I share this story, and you might be able to come up with some of your own, to illustrate how thinking about emotional responses to life events are constantly evolving. For someone of my grandmother's generation grief was an indulgence better managed by repression than expression.

We have already seen how the body has its own way of employing mechanisms to reduce awareness that allows us to somehow stumble through the most awful of times and keep functioning enough to at least survive. We learn in this state to prioritise survival. **Deb Dana** in her wonderful book *Polyvagal Exercises for Safety and Connection* describes how our autonomic nervous system is divided into three parts, each with its own set of protective actions: immobilisation, followed by fight and flight and lastly safety that allows for processing and change. In early grief we are often immobilised by shock, which can then change into fight and flight responses, followed by a need to make sense, as best we can, of what is happening. Dana reminds us that some of these responses come from very old parts of the brain designed to keep us in safe in more primitive situations than most of us currently face. It does not mean that once we unfreeze ourselves, we will all automatically start physically fighting with each other or running off – although we may well feel like it.

When Dalia first heard about the death of her husband she was not by his bedside. She was in a hospital corridor trying to buy some snacks from a vending machine because her mother was bringing the children in to visit their dad later and Dalia wanted to give them both something sweet and comforting to eat. A nurse came and took Dalia into a small room with two chairs, some fake flowers in a vase and a box of tissues on a small coffee table. A room set up for the worst kind of conversations to take place. The nurse told her, as kindly as she could that that Dan had died. Dalia's first response was to sit completely still. She then stood up and told the nurse that couldn't be right because she had just seen him less than ten minutes ago and he was poorly but not dead. She had talked to him. Dalia goes to leave the room, saying she must see her husband immediately and where are the doctors looking after him? In this brief and utterly dreadful conversation Dalia moves from a state of immobilisation to fight, flight responses when she argues that what the nurse has told her simply can't be true. She is prepared to fight her way out of the room and back to her husband's bedside. She demands to see other people who will make sense of this horror and confirm what she knows to be true, that there is no way her husband, her beloved Dan can be dead. Weeks later Dalia can only recall fragments of these moments and conversations. Her brain seeks to protect her by dissociating from memories too unbearable to recall.

Grief therapists hear many accounts of what it's like to receive the worst of news. The accounts are of course all different but there are some threads of similarity that might resonate with you if you have ever been in the position to hear the worst of all news. When I told my partner that our friend had died – by her own hand – all those years ago – he said 'No'. Contained within that single word was the protective belief that this simply couldn't be happening. Someone somewhere had made a mistake and the truth was that she was alive. I remember feeling horrible, disconnected from him because I instinctively knew the news was true and she was dead. I don't know why we reacted differently. Maybe I knew her better and therefore knew more of her emotional struggles in life. Maybe my partner is more predisposed to blocking out bad news. We have a running joke between us that he can forget any arguments we have because they are upsetting. The point is we reacted differently in the moment and yet when we both look back on that awful evening it has a quality of unreality for us both. Perhaps it is reasonable to conclude that our brains work to protect us to varying degrees from painful truths according to our capacity to cope with those truths. Our responses are also influenced by what else we know and our habitual ways of coping and responding to the hardest aspects of our lives. There are similarities and there are differences in how we respond to pain.

Dalia finds that in the first few weeks after Dan's death, she moves through life like a robot. She feels as if she is floating somewhere slightly above herself, watching herself do ordinary things like prepare meals for her children, work out what she is supposed to do and what is involved in organising a funeral. In the UK, https://www.gov.uk/when-someone-dies has a useful list that offers a step-by-step guide. Dalia has lots of conversations with people who ask her if there is anything they can do. Dalia has absolutely no idea what anyone might do or could do to help her so she just tries to smile and say thank you. If you are reading this and want to know how best to support someone in their grief, I think the key is to offer to do something specific. Dalia's neighbour takes the children to the park several times during those awful early days and Dalia appreciates this simple act of kindness not least because she doesn't have to think to ask for it herself. When people ask Dalia how she is doing she doesn't know how to answer because she doesn't know how she is doing, she is just being as best she can. It is impossible for her to offer a commentary on how she is, as this would require her to examine her feelings sufficient to drum up some kind of answer. This would be like touching a painful wound. Dalia keeps her 'wound' covered and can't bring herself to look at it. Another useful point for those of us wishing to support and be kind to the bereaved is not to ask how they are in general but instead to make our questions smaller and therefore easier and safer to answer. Instead of 'how are you' a loaded and difficult question to answer as we have seen, try 'how has the morning been for you so far?' or 'how are you doing today?'

These experiences of early grief, characterised as they often are by shock, alarm and dissociation, are not the same for everyone. Furthermore, they are not permanent states. Just as the brain seeks to protect us from the worst of our pain, in most cases it can't keep it up all the time. It is not unusual to experience bursts of reality that break through our protective shields. These can be horrifying as you can imagine, and also highly unpredictable. One of the things bereaved people can feel worried about is the very real possibility that something will unexpectedly pierce their emotional defences and expose their pain and distress to the world. It can be helpful if you find yourself in such a situation to have a few stock phrases up your sleeve that will allow you to quickly get away from people if you need to. A peculiar truth about most people is they find physical discomfort much easier to understand and less awkward to respond to than emotional pain so you can try saying you need to go outside for a moment and 'get some air' as this will swiftly get you out of lots of situations when you feel as if you are about to fall to pieces. Dalia gets used to doing this but still finds that the awful truth of Dan's death catches her when she least expects it. She notices that sometimes these moments of truth make her feel as if she wants to howl and cry in ways that the culture she lives in would most likely find very embarrassing and worrying to respond to. She also notices that sometimes it's not tears but rage that overcomes her. She goes to collect her children from school one day and overhears some of the adults moaning about their partners and how they have to badger them to get them to do things round the house. Dalia in that moment, would sacrifice years of her life to have Dan back with her so she could moan at him for not having fixed the hinge on the kitchen cupboard like he said he would. Every time Dalia goes to that cupboard now, she feels the pain of her loss as if someone has punched her in the chest and she can't breathe properly. Standing at the school gate listening to a fairly ordinary conversation intended to benignly bond people together in the challenges of bringing up little children and managing a household, she feels a rage she barely recognises overtake her. Dalia wants to shout and swear and push these people over. She fantasises about shouting in their faces to ask them if they know, even for just one second, how lucky they are to have their partners available to moan at? She then feels ashamed and guilty. What kind of person is she becoming? At some level Dalia knows she is being unreasonable and at another, the rage of loss churns and burns within her, making her dream about lashing out at people in ways her moral brain finds frightening to contemplate.

IS THE IDEA OF STAGES OF GRIEF A HELP OR A HINDRANCE?

I hope by now I am managing to establish that early grief is a pretty horrifying and unpredictable place to be. Which brings us to what might be described as the theoretical elephant in the room and that is the concept of the stages of grief. The completely brilliant Cariad Loyd, creator of *Grief Cast*, a podcast that examines the human experience of grief and death, drily and with perfect understatement describes herself as 'not a fan of the stages of grief'. Me neither. In case you aren't familiar with these stages of grief they are the work of Elisabeth Kubler-Ross writing in her book *On Death and Dying* in 1969.

To give the book its full title it is *On Death and Dying: What the Dying Have to Teach Doctors, Nurses, Clergy and Their Own Families*, which indicates, quite correctly, that the ideas are based on the experience of people who are themselves facing death, and not on the bereaved. My own view is that some of the ideas contained within this undoubtedly rather famous piece of work, are useful and I have no wish to entirely dismiss them. She talks about denial as a characteristic of early grief, and as we have established this mirrors my experience of working with hundreds of bereaved people over many years for whom the shock and distress, the sheer alarm of death, can set up a protective mechanism that refuses to fully accept what has happened, or to put it another way, to deny it. Denial, as we might say nowadays, can definitely be a thing.

What, in my experience at least, is definitely not a thing is the prescriptive nature of this work. I find myself almost reluctant to name the stages here because of this. But let's face it, a quick Google will give you hundreds of references to follow up so I might as well bite the bullet. The stages are: Denial, Anger, Bargaining, Depression and Acceptance. Kubler-Ross later added a couple more to include Shock and Testing Reality. I would like to explain what I think is problematic about this work, but at the same time if any of those things on the list speak to you, and I strongly suspect they will, then that is useful for you and I hope you will take what you can from it. As I've hinted, one of my problems is the prescriptive nature of the stages. People more learned than me say that Kubler-Ross never intended them to be used in such a prescriptive way. But that is what's happened. They have, for many people, become the blueprint of how grief is meant to be. And it's just not like that, it really isn't that simple. As we have seen, the protective blanket of shock and denial often a characteristic of early grief isn't failsafe. Things break though. Rage and pain and despair and fear can all come tumbling through the gaps in our defences at any given moment causing us, assuming we are in a position to do so, to desperately explain to other people that we 'need some air' before taking to the hills in an attempt to get away from the onslaught. Neat, tidy and predicable it is not. I have literally lost count of the amount of people I have worked with who have worried that they are doing grief 'wrong'. So powerful are these ideas about the stages of grief that the bereaved frequently give themselves a really hard time when their experience doesn't seem to match the list. I think perhaps this is one of the reasons why so many of us working in the field are not as Cariad Loyd says, a fan of the stages of grief. It is a grim and what feels like unnecessary addition to people's existing pain for them to worry that their feelings, their loss and the ways they are finding as best they can to survive and stay alive is somehow not what they should be doing.

The other problem I have with these ideas is as well as being a stick to beat ourselves with when our experience doesn't fit the proscription, is that they are everywhere! I read fiction books where someone is bereaved and before you know it, the stages of grief pop up. I mentioned previously what happens if you Google 'grief' I did it just now and the fourth result (which I won't reference) talks about the Stages of Grief and How to Heal. I have asked myself why these ideas have become so embedded in our understanding of grief and loss. My conclusions are that they offer a sanitised, safe version of the experience of bereavement that implies we will all move through the stages neatly and predictably to a point where we reach the point of 'Acceptance'. I wonder if we find what I would describe as the illusion of control, comforting. I wonder also if it is a comfort that offers more to us collectively than it does to the individually bereaved. What I mean by that is that those people standing at the school gate with Dalia, knowing that her husband has just died, perhaps find it comforting to believe that in time Dalia's pain will reduce and she will come to a place of 'acceptance'. Do the stages of grief ironically offer an opportunity to go into collective denial about the true horror and messiness and sheer excruciating pain of loss? Do most people, until it hits them, prefer to imagine grief is nothing like as dreadful as it actually is. Does this account not only for the popularity of these ideas but also for why the bereaved sometimes find themselves being treated as awkward pariahs to be avoided. Do we seek to deny and cling on to the comfort of neat and tidy stages because it is an attempt to reduce our fear of the unpredictable but inevitable truth of death?

WILL IT ALWAYS BE LIKE THIS?

The question posed at the beginning of this chapter was 'Will it always be like this?' and I have just spent the last few pages exploring with you what I find problematic about the idea of neat and tidy stages of grief that lead encouragingly to some point of resolution and acceptance of what has happened. So does this mean that the answer to the question is yes, it will always be like this and you just have to get on with it? Well, no. Like most things about living with grief it can be contradictory and rather complicated. My experience of all feelings, not just big feelings, but all feelings, large and small, are that they can change. But then again, I notice that some feelings don't change and importantly sometimes we don't want our feelings to change. It's all rather confusing. However I think taking our courage in our hands and exploring our feelings, no matter how contradictory they may be, is a really important part of what we can do to help ourselves survive and learn to live with our grief. Let's begin with an example of how feelings can change. Dalia used to feel really irritated with Dan when she asked him repeatedly to sort out the hinge on the kitchen cupboard and he never got round to it. Now she looks back on the times when she felt grumpy with him and it feels like she is touching a wound, the centre of the pain she feels about his death. She thinks of all the brilliant things Dan did when he was alive. How much he loved her and the kids, how he made them all laugh, how hard he worked. There are many wonderful and painful things for Dalia to remember about Dan. Then Dalia goes to open her cupboard door to get pasta out for the kid's supper and the hinge plays up again and Dalia feels that old irritation (because let's face it, the door is a nuisance) and she doesn't know whether to laugh or cry. Dalia gets exasperated with herself because although the door is tiresome there's a part of her that doesn't want it to be fixed because her irritation makes her feel more connected to a time when Dan was still alive. She feels all of these feelings all at once whilst doing her best to get on with making a meal for their children.

Dalia's feelings are complicated and contradictory. Sometimes they threaten to overwhelm her. At three in the morning whilst the children sleep and Dalia lies alone in the dark, she sometimes imagines that if she goes to sleep, she might die of a broken heart and simply never wake up again. Other times she pushes her feelings down and gets on with feeding her children. The fluctuating nature of feelings, the changes in their intensity and the unpredictable, contradictory turmoil of it all can be exhausting. Grieving people often experience a fatigue that is not based on the things they are doing. Sometimes it's an effort to do much of anything, because of the energy it takes to experience the interior world of grief.

I can offer my own example of how some feelings change and some feelings are ones I want to preserve and never let go of. When my friend took her own life, I was so angry with her. How could she do something so selfish was how my thinking went, when I could get my brain to work that is. When I look back, I don't remember having much clarity at that awful time. But some feelings have changed. I am no longer angry with her. I feel terribly sad for her and all the people who loved her that she never got to live out the rest of life and that dying seemed to her to be the only option. Death of this kind leaves many unanswered questions that you just have to learn to live with because there is no other choice. The feelings I want to hold on to are how brilliant she was, how funny and creative and spirited. I have specific memories that I deliberately re-visit to keep them fresh in my mind. I have a letter she wrote to me when I was having a difficult time and it's full of love and hope and tenderness. These experiences and the experience of so many people I have worked with have taught me that grief is not predictable. It doesn't present itself in neat and tidy stages to be worked through. Some things change, some things don't and we learn, somehow to grow around our grief.

Given that the stages of grief are undoubtedly such a popular way to try to understand grief and given that I have shared some of my reservations, do they have anything at all to offer us that might be useful? As with most things I have learned about grief there are no absolutes. Nor is grief one distinct feeling. It seems to me to be a complex tangle of shifting, sometimes contradictory feelings that can be very hard to recognise and understand. No wonder grieving people struggle to answer well-meaning questions about how they are. Sometimes the most honest answer might be 'I just don't know'. Anger is cited as a stage of grief and whilst I don't care for the idea of a distinct stage with a tidy beginning and end, I believe anger forms part of what many people experience when someone dies. Anger can be one of those feelings that people have a lot of trouble with. It is sometimes the feelings we have about feeling angry that can cause us problems rather than the anger itself.

IS ANGER PART OF MY GRIEF?

Let's start with the feelings we have about feeling angry. Dalia often feels angry with Dan. She never wanted to be a single parent. Bedtime is a bit of a nightmare now she is on her own. Her and Dan had a great routine, sharing the load, so each child got time with a parent, a bath and a bedtime story. Now it's much more difficult. Dalia frequently feels furious with Dan for leaving her on her own. She shouts at him in her head, asking him what the hell he was he thinking and where exactly is he when they all need him so badly. Dalia knows Dan is dead. Dalia can't believe she is never going to see Dan again. Dalia misses him dreadfully. Dalia is full of rage. All of these feelings co-exist alongside of one another and just to add to the mix Dalia then feels horribly guilty for feeling angry and stupid that she can't seem to accept that Dan is not going to pull up outside the house in his car and walk through the front door ever again. Dalia's feelings about her feelings make things even harder for her.

I wonder, how do you feel about being angry? Is it something you can allow yourself to feel? Do you feel guilty about it? Perhaps you are afraid of your own anger and what it might lead to? Most of us have feelings about the feeling of anger. When anger becomes part of our grief things can get really complicated. We will almost certainly be affected by our habitual response to anger. In common with a lot of people I often don't like angry me. She is sharp-tongued, she can be unkind and she can say things she doesn't mean. At the same time, I feel like I should be able to allow myself to be angry when my feelings are hurt or something seems wrong to me. In my work as a therapist, I often find it helpful to work with what is known as Internal Family Systems (IFS) which is a way to identify and work with different parts of the self. Alanis Morissette (a woman who knows a thing or two about anger if you have ever listened to her very famous album *Jagged Little Pill*) writes in the preface to one of my favourite books about IFS, Richard Schwartz's *No Bad Parts*, that through working with parts of herself she encountered her rage, shame, terrors, depressions, aches and yearnings. Her humiliations and her grief. The principle of working with different parts of the self and allowing those parts to be recognised rather than repressed is I believe a very helpful way to start to learn to live with one's grief and however that grief has chosen to present itself to you today. It is quite likely that in amongst the different feelings and parts of you that are activated through your grief there will be some anger. My suggestion is that it is useful to get to know all your feelings and what they have to teach you. Anger is one place to start with the process of getting to know our responses.

When you think of Dalia and how she sometimes feels angry at Dan for dying, how do you respond? Do you feel sympathetic towards her? Can you understand why she might feel like that? Or do you think her anger is unjustified as Dan didn't choose to die. Is she being unfair to him? Your feelings about Dalia may offer you some clues about how you feel about your own anger, if that is present for you. Are you kind to yourself about it or do you feel ashamed? Most of us are much harder on ourselves than we would ever be on someone else, even a fictional character in a book about living with grief. Can you give yourself permission to feel what you feel without punishing yourself or disguising your feelings? It can be a lot harder to do than it first appears. As we have already seen, anger, particularly anger with someone who has died, often comes with guilt. Can you find a way to separate yourself from the part of you that feels angry, enough to find out a bit more about why you are feeling like this?

Imagine if we could have a conversation with Dalia's anger. What might it say? I can envisage this part talking about how much she misses him and how it just isn't fair that their future together has been taken away. That their children have lost their father and will have to grow up without him. That she, Dalia, now has to do everything and it's really hard and really tiring. I can hear her saying how much she hates the cancer that ended Dan's life and what a good man he was. In her worst moments of fury, I can imagine Dalia raging that bad people doing bad things are allowed to live whilst her lovely husband had his life taken away from him. I can picture in my mind's eye how her anger might change a little as other feelings emerge. I can hear Dalia starting to acknowledge how frightened she is on her own and how she feels terrified that she won't be a good enough parent to the children. As her anger subsides – having been heard and acknowledged – I can imagine that the overwhelming sadness hidden behind all that anger, might start to show itself.

WHAT'S THE POINT OF LOOKING AT MY FEELINGS WHEN IT'S SO PAINFUL TO DO SO?

Some clients I have worked with in grief therapy have asked me what the point of examining their feelings is when it is so painful and difficult. Isn't it better to just try to get on with life and not keep going over and over things that ultimately can't be changed? Later on in this book we will have a look at something called the Dual Processing model of grief that basically suggests that the experience of grief is a confusing mixture of trying to get on with life and needing to allow the powerful and difficult feelings associated with loss to be felt and not always denied and repressed. For the moment though, let's stick with anger. What if you could have a conversation with your anger. How might that go? What do you think you would learn about why you feel angry. There is a good chance that if you do start to think about this you will begin to feel less guilty and a bit more understanding of yourself and therefore better able to live with how you feel. You might even gain insight into the functionality of your anger. Human beings are meaning-making creatures. We try to make sense of the things we experience. When things don't make sense to us one of our responses can be to cast around for reasons why. We might even look for things or people to blame. Deciding that our loved one has died because of something or someone else is a way of making sense of what has happened. Focussing our anger on something or someone else is a way to distance ourselves from the pain. We can have fantasy conversations with the people or institutions that we hold responsible for causing us such pain. These fantasy conversations allow us to be powerful and come out on top. Probably the exact opposite of the sense of powerlessness and helplessness we actually feel about dealing with our loss. I'm not saying that blaming something or someone else is never justified. Depending on the circumstances that may be a legitimate position to take. What I am saying is that emotionally it is worth being aware of why you might be feeling as you do, the functionality of your anger and whether it is serving you well.

HOW DO I BEST CARE FOR MYSELF IN THE EARLY DAYS OF LOSS?

As we reach the end of this first chapter, I want to suggest to you that there are things you can do to look after yourself as you begin to learn to live with grief. You might notice I am carefully avoiding using the phrase self-care, as for me this has become something I associate with the idea that if we follow a certain set of actions, we can float through life avoiding its messiness and pain. By all means have a bubble bath and light a candle if you feel like it but I want to offer some ideas that seek to address how you might begin to learn to live with some of the worst stuff life can throw at you. The first of these ideas is to re-iterate to you that the ultimate goal of living with grief is to get your head around the horrible truth of what's happened. No one can adapt to something they are pretending hasn't happened. But guess what? If it helps to pretend sometimes, then go right ahead. Just don't pretend all the time or you will never allow yourself to grow round your grief. In the first instance shock and alarm will probably protect you from the truth at least some of the time and that's OK. In fact, that's a normal part of the process. But sooner or later we have to learn to get to grips with our feelings. For a lot of us in grief, that will include feeling angry and looking for things and people to blame. It can help to give ourselves permission to feel whatever we need to feel and recognise the functionality of our feelings. Throughout this book I will be talking to you about the relationship you have with your own feelings, and this includes how easy it is for you to notice and name what you feel; what understanding you can develop about the purpose of your feelings and how you can live alongside some of the really difficult feelings associated with grief. When I was training as a therapist, I learned a simple exercise to name and recognise my feelings better. I have shared this with many clients since and I want to share it with you now. Without spending too much time on it, try to come up with three things you are feeling right now. What are these feelings? Now score them out of ten, one is low and ten is high. If any of the feelings are uncomfortable or painful, what simple thing could you do to reduce the number by one?

Here's my example so you can see how it works.

My first feeling is Hopeful. I want you to find some comfort and hope in these pages, that's why I am writing them. I'll give that a 9 and I don't want to reduce that feeling as it's fine to feel hopeful.

My second feeling is Sad. Writing about grief makes me feel sad, for you, for myself and for all the people that I have worked with struggling to deal with their grief. It's tough. I'll give it a 7 for me today. I don't actually want that feeling to go away either, as I think it is part of what it is to be a compassionate human being and I value that. Having said that, later this evening I plan to watch a bit of telly to take my mind off the sadness and maybe reduce it down to a 5.

My third feeling is Hungry. As I prepare to shut my computer off and finish for the day, I notice I am hungry. Really hungry actually, now I think of it, probably about an 8. There is a reason why I haven't noticed this before and it's because my brain has been busy with other things. Now there is enough space for me to notice what is going on for me and what I need. I can go and prepare myself a meal and that will take my hunger number down to zero before it starts to climb back up again in due course.

Have a go for yourself and see how you get on.

GLOSSARY

Autonomic nervous system A component of the peripheral nervous system that regulates involuntary physiological processes such as heart rate, blood pressure and breathing.

Stages of grief A theory devised by Kubler-Ross that defines a ordered set of distinct processes that comprise a grief response

FURTHER RESOURCES

https://cariadloyd.com/griefcast
https://www.gov.uk/when-someone-dies

REFERENCES

Dana, Deb. *Polyvagal Exercises for Safety and Connection*, 2020, Norton, p. 3.

Kubler-Ross, E. *On Death and Dying*, 1969, Macmillan.

Morissette, Alanis. 'Foreword', in Schwartz, Richard C., *No Bad Parts*, 2021, Penguin Random House, xiii.

Parkes, Colin Murray. *Bereavement: Studies of Grief in Adult Life*, 1972, Tavistock Publications, p. 50.

Tonkin, Lois. 'Growing around grief: Another way of looking at grief and recovery', 1996, *The Australian Journal of Grief and Bereavement*, a.k.a. *Bereavement Care*, 15 (1): 10.

2

NO MORE CASSEROLES – WHAT HAPPENS NEXT?

- What happens when the shock wears off?
- What are the 'rules of grief' – either one's own or other people's?
- How can I use emotional insight to find out my own way of doing grief?
- How can I explain my feelings to other people?
- How long does grief last?

WHAT HAPPENS WHEN THE SHOCK WEARS OFF?

In case you are wondering what casseroles have to do with grief let me explain – and for those of you unfamiliar with what a casserole is, try stew! The point is that sometimes, soon after someone dies, there can be offers of help that take the form of people making the bereaved a casserole (or stew) for their freezer because that seems like a kind thing to do and often people have little idea what else to offer that might help. Bereaved people usually know that nothing will help if we understand help to be something that can change the truth of what has happened, but sometimes it is nice to receive kindness from others if it is offered, and difficult when those kind gestures dry up.

This was how it was for George. George thinks of himself as an ordinary kind of man. He was 76 when Pat, his wife of 51 years, died. Both he and Pat had assumed when they talked about it, which wasn't very often, that George would die before Pat. Pat had always looked after herself, eaten a good diet, gone to her weekly keep fit classes and only enjoyed the occasional glass of wine. George on the other hand used to drink too much, by his own admission, when he was younger. He used to smoke, and have a tremendous fondness for Pat's baking. So, when Pat was diagnosed with heart disease they were both shocked. Pat had noticed herself getting more tired and short of breath but thought that was just part of the natural ageing process and nothing to worry about. It was only when she found herself unable to look after the house and walk their dog, Maisie, that she started to worry. The diagnosis was followed by a regime of medication to manage her blood pressure and thin her blood. In the end, Pat was out in the garden when she had a heart attack and died. George had been out shopping and came home ready to make them both a cup of tea. He saw Pat lying on the grass in the garden, still wearing her gardening gloves. The paramedics summoned by George knew Pat was dead when they saw her and the doctor at the local hospital where Pat was taken confirmed cause of death as a heart attack or 'myocardial infarction' as it said on her death certificate.

In the first dreadful few weeks after Pat died, George received lots of offers of help and was asked by all sorts of people if he needed anything. George and Pat lived in a bungalow in a quiet cul-de-sac where they knew most of their neighbours. They had moved there when Pat turned 70 thinking this would be the house they would live in until they died. So, it proved it to be but much, much earlier than either of them had ever imagined. George was not only horribly shocked by Pat's death but also angry. He often thought about what a good woman she had been and what she might ever have done to deserve to die before her time, as he saw it. George would hear tentative knocks on his door and when he opened it to find various things for him to eat left on the porch floor, prepared by kind neighbours who weren't sure what else they could do. George ate the food because it was his habit not to waste things. He thanked people when he saw them or went round to return the dishes and plates that didn't belong to him. He always said he was doing all right when people asked. He literally had no words to describe what he really felt and he didn't want to share his feelings anyway. After a few weeks the knocks became less frequent. The funeral came and went and neighbours would see George out and about, walking Maisie or going to and from the shops, and assume that he was doing as well as could be expected and leave him to it.

The truth of how George is really feeling is complicated. There is a part of George that would quite like to go out for a few pints and have a chat with some of the men he knows from their local pub but he feels he can't do that because it is too early. George doesn't want people to think that he didn't care about Pat when he cared very much indeed. George thinks Pat is the only woman he ever properly loved. He had a couple of girlfriends before he met Pat but none who were important to him. During their long marriage George remained faithful to Pat even in his head. They had loved each other and in the last few years of their marriage, since they both gave up work, had been very happy in each other's company. Life had been good. But now George is lonely and misses the company of other people, but can't quite bring himself to do anything about this because it just doesn't seem right to him.

Sometimes George is plagued with guilt. He imagines himself to be a horrible person who selfishly only thinks of himself. How can he be contemplating going out and enjoying himself when his wife has only just died? He even feels guilty if he sees something amusing on television and finds himself laughing. Equally bewildering to George is how his moods and feelings can change without warning. One minute he's thinking about going out for a pint and the next he can barely imagine what the point of getting out of bed ever again might be. He is relieved he has Maisie, their whippet, who needs a walk every day even though she is, like most whippets, notoriously enthusiastic about lying around not doing much. George finds looking after Maisie comforting because he knows what he should be doing and tries to make sure he does what's right. In the rest of his life George feels like he has no clue as to what he should be doing.

He often feels like he is getting things really wrong. He tries to keep the house like Pat did but struggles to maintain her standards and then feels like he has failed her. At other times he sits around in a level of mess that would have horrified Pat because he just can't be bothered to get up and do anything.

George and Pat had one child; they wanted more but it wasn't to be. Their daughter Abbey lives a couple of hundred miles away but stays in touch. George knows he should be glad to hear from Abbey. George is part of a family WhatsApp group that Pat used to enjoy. Abbey and her partner post things, as do their grandchildren and George's sister Ruth who lives up in Scotland. George actually dreads the WhatsApp messages. He feels very confused about what he should and shouldn't be saying. Abbey worries if she thinks her dad is not going out and seeing people but was also audibly surprised and upset when George told her he had been thinking about donating some of Pat's things to the local hospice charity shop where Pat used to volunteer. George was only considering doing this doing this because he thought Pat would be pleased her things went to the shop that she enjoyed working in. Abbey's response made him feel guilty and tired and sad. He knows she is dealing with her own grief and worries about him. The more he hides his real feelings from her, the greater the gap between them seems to grow. George knows Pat wouldn't want that but he doesn't know what he can do about it. Should he be trying to carry on as normal when nothing feels normal anymore? George wonders if he will feel like this for the rest of his life and how long that will be. Sometimes he feels like a much younger man again, not in a good way but worried, uncertain and not sure what the rules of life are that he should be following. At 76 having just lost his wife, this feels very tough indeed.

WHAT ARE THE 'RULES OF GRIEF' – EITHER ONE'S OWN OR OTHER PEOPLE'S?

If we stop for a moment to consider George and his struggle to understand what he should and shouldn't be doing and feeling, we might wonder where these 'rules' are coming from. Before Pat died George hadn't spent much time thinking about how people behave after someone important has died. Now it is something that causes him a lot of anxiety and distress as if he didn't have enough to deal with already. It might be useful to stop and consider if you are aware of any of your own rules or those of the people around you that might be governing how you understand and experience your own grief. It is likely that all of us are influenced by a whole range of variables, for example how old we are; whether we adhere to any particular religious or spiritual beliefs and customs; what part of the world we live in; our cultural identity and so on. One of the first things I learned when I began my work as a grief therapist is that everybody's grief is different. On balance this is a belief I have stuck with over the years but nonetheless I have also had many conversations with clients about how difficult it is to work out how to grieve when there are no clear rules or guidelines. Honouring difference seems like a laudable goal but it does sometimes leave people wondering if how they are feeling is OK. As we see with George, life can become difficult when it feels as if there are rules, some of which you weren't even aware of until it seems like you are transgressing them without even meaning to. Grief is confusing, that's for sure.

George was born in 1948. Julia Samuels in her book *Grief Works* suggests that the generation born before the 1960s was brought up to be self-reliant and view mental distress as a weakness. Perhaps we can see some of this playing out in George's feelings about himself. However, some of the internal rules we can find ourselves living with or indeed struggling with can be much harder to pinpoint. They aren't just to do with when we were born. There is a branch of psychoanalytic theory called Transactional Analysis, often referred to as TA. TA teaches that for many of us an unconscious plan, formed in our childhood and heavily influenced by our parents or carers, can become a way of life, or as TA calls it a Life Script. Life Scripts can be tricky. They can become a covert set of rules we are barely aware of but that influence our behaviour often in unhelpful or restrictive ways. In addition to a Life Script, TA also suggests that our very understanding of who we are and what we are like can be influenced by what our parents and carers tell us about ourselves. If you think of your own early life perhaps you can recall how you were described by parents, carers, teachers and so on when you were growing up. Were you the 'shy one' or the 'clumsy one'? Were you 'naughty' or 'good'? Whilst these labels may be rooted in a degree of truth (and sometimes not) they can become a self-fulfilling prophesy as children grow up and formulate their understanding of who they are. TA calls the process of describing a child to a child as an Attribution, these can become part of your Life Script, along with something called an Injunction. An Injunction is a rule or restriction that our parents can sometimes communicate to us, either consciously or unconsciously.

Thinking about George, we can't know what his Life Script might be or whether it has served him well or badly. Generally, the idea of a Life Script is that it is better to bring it into conscious awareness. This way it stops being a set of rules that we find ourselves living by that don't necessarily allow us to be fully the people we are meant to be. It gives us the opportunity to decide for ourselves what rules, values and so on we want to try and live by. Neither George or Pat thought much about how to deal with the death of the other and simply got on with the business of enjoying their lives together. Now Pat has died George is experiencing unexpected and sometimes conflicting feelings of guilt and anxiety about how he is living with his grief. You might notice that this is in addition to George's actual feelings of grief. Instead, these are feelings about how he is doing grief and whether it is OK or not. Perhaps we can imagine that some of George's 'rules' might be influenced by things he was told about himself when he was very young. What if George came home from school one day crying having been tripped up and cut his knee by one of the older children. His mother, finding her own distress at George's tears difficult to cope with, might have told him he was too soft and needed to toughen up a bit in an attempt to not only protect George from future harm but also protect herself from having to witness his distress. If the idea that he was too soft became an Attribution and the instruction to toughen up a bit became an Injunction, then that might, even now, years later, be influencing how George is feeling about his grief and sadness that Pat has died. He might feel a vague sense of unease that he is taking it too hard. He might try to carry on as 'normal' even though he isn't quite sure what that means anymore. Confusingly, he might also find himself feeling guilty of trying to get on with his life when Pat was not given that choice. Can you see how George might be falling into an old Life Script – that he is too soft and needs to toughen up a bit – that doesn't serve him very well in what is an unimaginably painful part of his life. Pushing his feelings down and pretending they aren't there won't be very helpful to him and will make him feel uneasy when he attempts to try to do what those old rules would have him believe are the right way to go.

I hope you are becoming more aware of how what I have called the 'rules' of grief can ultimately make life even harder at a time when most of us would welcome anything that might offer us some respite from the pain. If you want to read more about TA there are plenty of books on the subject and quite a few short YouTube videos you can watch. I have included some suggestions in the reference sections of this book. It can be useful to develop a radar about your own and others rules about grief so that you can become more aware of them and decide for yourself if they seem kind, sensible and likely to support you. None of us have to follow a Life Script full of ideas about who we are and how we should be. We can figure these things out for ourselves but it does take some thinking about.

HOW CAN I USE EMOTIONAL INSIGHT TO WORK OUT MY OWN WAY OF DOING GRIEF?

A way to develop or improve the functioning of your own emotional radar is to try to identify and name all the feelings you are experiencing. However, when we are overwhelmed with strong and difficult feelings this can be challenging, and you might wonder how it will help or even worry that it will make things worse. to At the end of

Chapter 1 I encouraged you to have a go at the three feelings exercise. For this to be of continued benefit you need to do it regularly, not just once. The more used to noticing and naming your own feelings you become the better you will get at it. As for making things worse, I absolutely believe there is a time and a place for distraction from painful feelings. It makes sense to me to seek out safe ways to reduce pain if we can, to give ourselves a break from time to time. I say safe because we all know there are some very effective options for numbing feelings in the world we live in, drugs, alcohol and excessive gambling to name just three that ultimately develop their own dreadful momentum until they are controlling us and harming us. Approach with caution is my thought, and try to find safe ways that suit you to switch off as best you can when that feels the right thing to do.

However, switching off painful feelings all of the time is generally not a great idea when it comes to learning to how to live with grief. It is really hard to learn to live with something we prevent ourselves from becoming familiar with and getting the measure of. In my practice as a therapist, I have sometimes asked a client to imagine there is an absolutely awful monster that has just come into the room and is now standing a few steps behind them. The rule is the client is not allowed to look round. I then tell the client that the monster has taken quite a large step towards them but they still mustn't look round. Most clients I have done this exercise with notice that their imagination is capable of conjuring up truly awful ideas about what the monster must be like. At the end of the exercise, I invite the client to look round and happily they see that there is no monster. We then relate this to the concerns we can have about looking at our feelings, especially when our feelings are indeed monstrous ones like grief and sadness and fear and longing. You know the drill. The message of the exercise is that it can be much worse not to look at our feelings and let them build up into something truly terrifying than it is to take a look and begin to understand what some of these feelings might be. Most people experience it as a relief. It doesn't make the feelings go away but there is a sense of at least knowing a bit more about what you are dealing with which allows you start to figuring out what might help you and what you need.

Let's imagine that you decide to go along with this as an idea. How might you begin not only to discover what you feel but whether there are any of those pesky rules we have talked about that are making life even harder for you than it already is (if that's possible). A way of doing this is to use the word AND. This is how to do it:

If I think back to when I found out my mother had died, I had one big ball of feelings that was very tough to unravel. We had been estranged at my choice for many years, in itself a horribly tough life decision that broke some rules for me about duty and what I should be doing and feeling.

I began by asking myself what I noticed I was feeling, ending each feeling with the word AND. It went something like this:

I feel completely shocked that she has finally died

AND

In a way I'm relieved

AND

I feel weird and awful for feeling that

AND

It's not surprising I feel that

AND

I remember loving her so much when I was little

AND

The pain of realising she didn't love me back in the same way is still awful

AND

I've been living with this most of my life

AND

I'm tired and sad and just need time to get my head round all of this

Can you see how using the word AND after each sentence helped me to drill down into a complex mess of feelings, acknowledge the contradictions, and be aware of any unhelpful rules – mine were about it being wrong to feel relieved and guilty that I had chosen not to see her. It helped me figure out a bit about what I needed: rest, time and no pressure to do anything except get used to the truth of her death and try to be compassionate towards myself.

Let's try it with George:

George feels overwhelmingly sad that Pat has died

AND

He is shocked as he thought they both had years left together

AND

He's angry that she has died when she was so healthy and kind

AND

He feels guilty that he is alive and she isn't

AND

He would sometimes quite like to get on with life again

AND

Sometimes he's not sure he can learn to live without her

AND

He doesn't want to make things worse for his daughter

AND

He worries that he is still that little boy who was too soft and needed to toughen up a bit

AND

He kind of knows that's stupid and unhelpful

AND

Now he's fed up about thinking about his feelings

We can see that for George the word AND allows him to feel things that don't make sense and takes the pressure off him to feel one simple thing at a time because life and grief are just not like that. It even allows him to notice his early attribution of being too soft and the injunction to toughen up, and decide that these old ideas are not helpful for him now. At the end of the exercise, it allows George to recognise that he has done enough self-reflection for the moment and instead think about what he needs in the moment. George is

British so the chances are that's probably a cup of tea. I would like to invite you to try the AND exercise for yourself; tea afterwards is of course optional.

The title of this chapter is 'No More casseroles – what happens next?' and whilst you may or not have received any actual casseroles it might be worth thinking about how you can use what you are learning. It can help you to get support from others if it is available and explain how you are feeling to anyone who might be worrying about you. I'm conscious as I write this that grief is horribly isolating and you may be reading this thinking that no-one cares enough to be worrying about you. If that's how it is for you then I am truly sorry. Brace yourself because you may not like the next bit. If you are feeling completely alone then the only person who can do something about that is you. I appreciate none of us can magic up an instantly loving family or crowds of supportive friends but we can take small steps towards making connections with others. I know this because I have seen it in action. Remember those many thousands of hours of bereavement counselling I have offered to others? Well, the fact is that as well as that being a process I very much hope was helpful for them, it was also extremely helpful to me and taught me most of what I have learned about living with grief.

I have watched overwhelmingly sad and sometimes shy people learn to go for a morning walk and start nodding at people they see along the way. I have seen people who felt their life was over and who really weren't sure if they wanted to live or die find ways to struggle back to their lives and start to make connections with people and engage in activities they found diverting. A lot of this is based on having a word with your inner child (we all have one) and explaining as kindly as you can that you can't have what you really want – often that will be that your person didn't die – and you have to find ways to live with that as the title of this book implies. It is one of the great challenges of adulthood that we all have to get to grips with the fact we can't always have what we want, as I mentioned to you in Chapter 1.

HOW CAN I EXPLAIN MY FEELINGS TO OTHER PEOPLE?

With the tough but true idea in mind that this new reality is what you are now left with, no matter how unwelcome and painful it might be, it makes sense to me for us to learn more about what we are feeling. We can use that information to help ourselves and where possible help others to help us or at least understand something of what we are going through. A word of caution at this point. I have learned that most of us crave the BIG solution. The thing that will make the pain go away and significantly change our reality. Not only do we want the BIG solution we also want it NOW. Sadly, this is another one of those things we can't have. You might ask yourself, as I have asked many clients in the past, that if you could find a way to wave a magic wand and instantly feel better but the price of that magic spell is you lose all your memories of the person who has died, would you go for it? Nearly everyone I've asked says no. Perhaps then, it is true that, as Colin Murray Parkes said, 'Grief is the price we pay for love' A price that apparently most of us are willing to pay it if we get to retain our memories that are of course part of the love we still feel. I wonder if you are beginning to formulate a sense in your own mind that at least some of what you are feeling right now is not going to go away. The challenge of grief really is to learn to live alongside it. If you are, then that is a difficult but useful place to begin working out what you feel, what you need and how you might describe these things to someone else should you choose to.

For George as he works his way through his feelings, a few things are beginning to emerge. Here are three of the insights that George has had about his life now, as he tries to figure out how to live without Pat:

Insight 1

George feels sad. He misses Pat. Sometimes these feelings are very loud and pretty much all he can think about. At other times they are more like a quiet hum in the background but they are always there.

Insight 2

George notices that it is very hard to predict when the feelings will get noisier or quieter. He worries about making a fool of himself when he is out and about in case the feelings suddenly start to become unexpectedly loud.

Insight 3

These feelings of sadness and loss are not, by a long way, the only feelings that George is experiencing. He can also feel angry, sad, restless, resentful, exhausted and even bored with feeling so miserable. He feels these things (and others) alongside of his sadness and loss, and sometimes it makes no sense to him at all.

Let's look at these three feelings in turn and consider what George might do to respond helpfully and compassionately to each of them. It might also help him to explain them to someone else and get some support. Before we do that, I'd like to ask you to remember what I said about most of us wanting big solutions and wanting them now. Can we try to accept that this just isn't possible and be mindful not to discount smaller things we might do? It's easy to dismiss the little things precisely because they are little and they won't make the big things go away any time soon. In my practice as a therapist, I often refer to this as the 'wiggle room', that tiny bit of space between you and a feeling or situation that you can do something about no matter how small and pointless we might be inclined to think of it. Wiggle room is all we've got to work with here so don't dismiss it.

Things George can do:

Insight 1

He can change his performance criteria. George is not failing at grief if he always feels the sadness of his loss. That's just how it is for him.

Insight 2

George can give himself permission to leave a situation either temporarily or permanently if he feels uncomfortable or overwhelmed by emotion. He can learn to expect the unexpected and accept that grief is impossible to predict and that's just the nature of the thing.

Insight 3

George can use his developing awareness to notice he feels contradictory things at the same time. He can try to stop judging this as ridiculous or strange. He can use scaling (marking the intensity of the feeling out of ten) to see how they stack up in comparison to one and other.

What can George tell other people to get support and help them understand him a bit more?

Insight 1

He can find a simple description for how he feels that others might understand. For example:

'I have good days and bad'. If George explain this to his daughter, the next time he is confronted with the family WhatsApp group and he's having a bad day he can simply say:

'Today's not been an easy one'. This means he doesn't have to pretend but it also signals that not every day is the same as that.

Insight 2

George can prepare some exit strategies in social situations that will allow him to make a swift exit if he feels he might start crying or in his words 'making a fool of himself'. Do you recall the idea of explaining that you need a breath of fresh air that I talked about in Chapter 1?

George can take this further and warn people in advance that this might happen. He can use phrases that explain, without going into unnecessary details, that he sometimes needs to 'take 5 minutes'.

Insight 3

If George chooses to share his inner turmoil to any degree, he can say

> Half the time I don't know what I'm going to feel. I have to just go with the flow.

Now might be a good time to check in with yourself.

- What insights are emerging for you about your grief?
- What might your wiggle room be to respond kindly and compassionately to yourself?
- What might you choose to share with others?

And finally… what might you be discounting as pointless because they are not BIG solutions?

HOW LONG DOES GRIEF LAST?

I wonder what you make of this question and what your initial response might be? My experience is people can feel a bit shifty about asking this of themselves never mind admitting to someone else that they would quite like to know what they are in for. What do you feel? Have you thought about it? And if you have what's your best guess? Or does it seem daft to even imagine that how you feel now could ever change. I spent quite a lot of time in Chapter 1 explaining why I don't find the idea of stages of grief particularly useful. Doesn't this imply that grief stays the same and how you feel now is how you are going to feel for the rest of your life? Here's where I am glad I'm a therapist, as in my opinion anyway this has given me license to begin this paragraph about a question with another question back to you (therapists love doing this – it's one of our things).

However, given that you have been interested enough to read this far I'm also going to defy type and have a crack at answering this as best I can. It's not simple. Beware people who tell you things about timescales. I have heard all sorts of things in my career. Here are some examples:

- The first year and all the first anniversaries – birthdays, Christmas, anniversary of the death itself and so on – are the hardest
- 'Normal grief' takes about two years to work through. Any longer than that and it becomes 'Complex grief'
- The older you are the harder it is to cope with loss and change
- The younger you are the more grief affects your emotional development
- Time is a great healer

I'm not saying all the above is a load of rubbish, far from it. If you find truth in all or any of those ideas then that is worth paying attention to. The key here is that you have to assess for yourself what seems to fit and what doesn't. My problem lies with the idea that there is a universal, one-size-fits-all truth about grief, including what it's meant to be like and how long it might last. This seems ridiculous to me. I prefer to think of each individual grief as a unique reflection of the relationship the griever had with the deceased. This seems to echo the many examples of grief I have had the privilege to hear about in my work. It also explains why different people will grieve differently for the same person, because their relationship with that person was different.

In addition to my own idea (and I'm not alone with this) that grief is as different as each individual relationship is different, there is an implied belief in many recognised theories about grief that your actions can influence how you experience your grief. This whole book is based on the premise that there are things you can do to help yourself learn to live with grief and therefore by implication there may be things you can do or not do that might make living with grief even more difficult than it already is. So, my answer in short is that I believe two things about grief:

It changes.

You can do things to help or hinder those changes.

I don't think it ever goes away though, not really. When I think of my own losses and how I feel about them I notice that there is a sense of wounds that have largely healed over but have certainly left scars and weaknesses. I know that some of those wounds can re-open again, get infected and become very painful. I have realised I can learn how to look after myself and not do things to make it worse. I also know that sometimes I actively want to connect with the rawness of an open wound because even though it is terribly painful it is a way of feeling close to the object of my loss. I am wary of any ideas about grief that seem to me to be too prescriptive. You might have figured out already that I'm not too keen on rules and expectations about grief. I have seen too many people giving themselves a hard time about whether their grief is OK and if they doing it right. It's the ultimate double whammy of pain that people have to first of all deal with their losses and then deal with anxiety and doubt about how they are responding and if they are doing grief right. If I had one message that has underpinned all my work as a grief therapist that I would like to pass on to you, it's that you have to do grief your way and that therefore is the only right way to do it.

To return to the question of how long grief lasts, maybe a sensible response is to say that it's impossible to predict because it's as unique as the relationship it is based on. What we can say is that it changes and we, therefore have to change with it. At least some of how we experience our grief is going to be dependent on how we respond to the need to change. It's a difficult one because for most of us we are not changing because of a positive thing – like winning the lottery. Instead, we are faced with having to change, to adapt and to learn to live with something we never wanted and often don't want to face up to because it's just so painful. Even when death comes as a relief or when the relationship we have had has been catastrophically damaging to us, such as when an abuser dies, there can be grief. Grief for what happened, what could never be pain free and what we couldn't fix or confront. Certainly, when my own mother died, I found myself grieving for the mother I remembered as a tiny child, so glamorous and full of fun or so it seemed to me, and the mother

I didn't have as I got older and our relationship broke down so comprehensively. It seems there is no escaping grief and perhaps we can begin to acknowledge that it's a good thing that it changes even if it is impossible to predict quite how it changes. Can we acknowledge that allowing grief to change even to the smallest degree might be a way of learning to live with it?

When considering the question of what we can do to help ourselves learn to live with our grief and step back from it just enough to allow it and therefore us to change, I find it helpful to differentiate between grief and memories. Before this chapter ends and we say goodbye to George I'd like to re-visit him one more time to explore the difference between these two things a bit more. When Pat first died George struggled with everything in the home that reminded him of her. Given that they lived together for over 50 years, this was pretty much everything. Even things she didn't like or have much to do with remind him painfully of her. In his mind he plays the scene when he came home from the shops and saw her lying dead on the lawn, over and over again. He doesn't purposely summon the images, in fact he tries not to think about it as it's just so dreadful, but the images come anyway. He wakes up in the night and can't get back to sleep because when he closes his eyes all he sees is his Pat, lying lifeless in her beloved garden. It is horrifyingly grim. If you recognise any of these experiences as being similar to something you are going through then my heart goes out to you. If, over time, these images are still intense and intrusive, then you might consider talking to your GP or seeking out a grief therapist. I can't tell you how long is too long – although others may disagree – but I can urge you to exercise judgment on this and take professional advice if you feel you need to.

George finds it very hard to look at photographs of Pat although he forces himself to do so because he wants there to be some nice pictures of her to display at her funeral. In those very early days of George's grief, he struggles to remember much of anything except that last dreadful day and what happened subsequently. Even then his memory is fragmented and confused. Over time though, he finds himself remembering other things. Usually, the memories come unbidden or because of some trigger or other. It might be something someone says, or a song he hears that reminds him of her. Sometimes it is hard to fathom quite what has brought her so vividly to mind, it just seems to happen. Mostly George feels overwhelmed with sadness when this happens. He cries himself to sleep some nights and at other times he feels like his mind is being taken over by memories of her and he wishes he could think of something else because it's all so sad and tiring for him. It seems to George that he is never going to be able to remember the happy times with Pat because to do so is to become overwhelmed with emotion. There is an incident at the local library when George goes to take Pat's books back and pay the fine despite managing to tell the librarian that Pat has died which is why the books are overdue. The librarian says she is very sorry for his loss but he must have so many lovely memories to look back on. George feels like punching her. He doesn't because George is not a violent man and is in fact quite shocked at his thuggish fantasy. He ruminates on this as he walks home. Is this what he has become? A man who fantasises about attacking librarians just because they are a bit tactless.

HOW LONG DOES GRIEF LAST?

I talked earlier about grief and loss being like wounds. It might help us to understand not just George's feelings in those early days after Pat died, but our own too. The wounds are new. They are raw and easily infected. Everything around the wound is tender and we have to stay vigilant to make sure things heal as they should do. If not, we may need to seek help. The analogy is a useful one to help understand why, to begin with, memories are so excruciatingly painful and raw. Over time though the wound very gradually begins to heal and we become accustomed to this new way of being. We realise that the wound will leave a permanent scar and we will never forget. That can be a comfort. Slowly it becomes possible for us to access happier memories. George finds he can look at some of his photographs without always breaking down into tears. Sometimes he finds he has tears in his eyes and can smile at the same time. Some of Pat's things that in the beginning he could barely bring himself to acknowledge become very precious. He eventually does manage to donate some of her clothes to charity. His daughter takes some things that Pat wanted her to have. The grandchildren come to visit and choose some things they want to remind them of granny. George knows that some things he will keep forever because he wants to and they have become some of the most valuable things he owns. For George, over time, he is able to separate out his memories from his pain just enough to take an albeit poignant and bittersweet pleasure in those memories and there is comfort to be had in remembering.

In this way, and in others too many to fully explore here, George is changed by the death of Pat and he sometimes grudgingly, and sometimes less so, allows those changes to become part of him. You may be familiar with the character of Miss Havisham. She is a character created by the writer Charles Dickens and appears in his book *Great Expectations*. Having been jilted on her wedding day Miss Havisham shuts herself away. She stops all the clocks, only ever wears her wedding clothes and leaves the wedding feast to rot. I think it's fair to say that whilst nobody died Miss Havisham is a good example of someone whose way of living with grief is to actively prevent as many changes as she can. Suffice to say Miss Havisham ends up extremely bitter and sad. Remember the two things I told you I believe about grief. That it changes and that you can do things to help or hinder those changes. I hope these ideas are starting to give you some strategies for how you are going to learn to live with your grief and ideally avoid becoming like Miss Havisham.

I would like to suggest that you take things as slowly as you need to. There is no timeline here as to when you should look at a photograph or allow a memory to give you a tiny amount of pleasure. The important thing is that you pay attention to what you are feeling and keep developing a compassionate awareness of self. Let that be your guide to what happens next when all those casseroles imagined or real – stop turning up on your doorstep.

GLOSSARY

Transactional Analysis A theory of personality developed by Eric Berne.

Life Scripts A set of rules we develop about how life is based on our early experiences and decisions

Injunctions internalised and often unspoken negative messages that children absorb from parents, carers and other authority figures

Attributions Statements made about a person often in childhood that significantly impact their understanding and beliefs about who and how they are

FURTHER RESOURCES

Injunctions. https://www.youtube.com/watch?v=QNjdNOaS8Zw
TA life script explained. https://www.youtube.com/watch?v=FKEFgm0R0Sc

REFERENCES

Samuels, Julia. *GriefWorks*, 2017, Penguin Random House, p. 44.

Stewart, I. and Joines, V. *TA Today – A New Introduction to Transactional Analysis*, 1987, Lifespace Publishing.

3

WHAT IS THE DARK SIDE OF GRIEF?

- Is it normal to have such terrible feelings?
- How can I learn to deal with the worst of my feelings?
- Why do I feel so many different and often completely unexpected things?
- Some of my thoughts are very strange; am I losing grip on my own reality?
- How can I keep myself safe?
- Why do I feel so guilty if I ever feel anything except sad?
- Is it OK to sometimes just feel numb?

IS IT NORMAL TO HAVE SUCH TERRIBLE FEELINGS?

We have already established that feeling angry is often part of grief. Unsurprising when you stop to consider that anger can be a response to feeling that something terribly unfair and cruel is happening. It can come when we feel powerless and helpless to do anything or change anything. It can also come as a very powerful shield behind which other more vulnerable feelings can be hidden. C. S. Lewis wrote a book called *A Grief Observed* after his wife died when they had only been married four years. It was originally published under a pseudonym in 1961. It's now considered to be a classic of its kind and we can take our cue from some of his extraordinary wisdom to notice that he found it helpful to step back from his grief, and notice how he felt. He also gave himself permission to allow as many feelings as he could to come to the surface, be acknowledged, named and in his case written about. We can learn from this and from his many insights into what grief was like for him. A much-quoted example of this was Lewis' observation that grief can be a lot like fear. When I think of the procession of broken, desolate people I have worked with over the years I am struck by their collective courage to gradually learn to face the worst of their feelings. They discovered that the power of their feelings to harm them and prevent them from learning to live with grief is often rooted in silence. How did those people so broken by grief and loss learn to put themselves back together sufficiently to be able to continue to live with grief? How can you learn to do the same?

First, let's state the obvious: none of this is easy! You have to pick your moment. There will be times when you simply cannot do what we therapists like to call 'The Work'. My thought is don't even try. On those days you focus on keeping your head above the water line. You tell yourself to keep breathing in and out and you wait. You will know when the moments come. You might even feel guilty and uncomfortable when they do – we will come back to that. But when they do arrive no matter how tentatively and shakily, I invite you to ask yourself what you are feeling. Really work on noticing the feelings behind the feelings. Like the exercise I talked about in Chapter 2, use the word AND to try to notice what you feel AND what else you feel. Be curious about what might be hidden behind bigger noisier feelings like anger and outrage. C. S. Lewis suggested that for him fear was hidden behind his feelings of anger. I wonder what else might have been there for him and might be there for you?

I'd like you meet Jaden. Jaden, like C. S. Lewis, only had four very happy years with his partner before he died an untimely death due to a tragic accident whilst he was out riding his motorbike. Jaden's partner Michael loved his motorbike and was a very proficient rider.

The day he died he had been riding down a quiet country road when a car pulled out of a side turning at speed and crashed into Jaden. The driver, who was later found to be over the legal blood alcohol limit for driving, survived. Michael, however, died at the scene.

Jaden is a peace-loving man. Both his politics and his nature disincline him from thinking violence solves anything. At school Jaden was bullied for his sexuality as a young gay man. Like most gay men he has suffered from name calling, intimidation and other kinds of prejudice. Jaden has learned how to keep his head down and walk away from trouble. Michael was the same. Their shared beliefs in kindness to their fellow human beings and education rather than brutality as a way to develop a more inclusive society were some of the many things that connected them. Now though, Jaden would like to kill the man who was driving the car that killed Michael. He literally can't stop thinking about it. When he is out in his own car and he sees a car that is the same colour or make as the car that killed Michael, he thinks about putting his foot down and smashing in to them. He lies awake at nights having horrible fantasies of revenge where he tears Michael's killer limb from limb. He wants to hurt him very badly indeed. He thinks about finding people this man cares about and hurting them. He is filled with the most exhausting and horrifying rage. Jaden doesn't recognise himself. He sometimes thinks about what Michael would say if he knew the thoughts that constantly turn over in his mind. He thinks that Michael would be appalled and even afraid of Jaden. This makes him howl with grief like an animal fatally wounded and unable to help himself.

It occurs to Jaden that he is handling Michael's death badly. He feels ugly and angry and out of control. He hides his feelings as he fears that were he to admit them to people they would pull away from him and he would be even more alone than he already feels himself to be. If he is really honest, he is disgusted with himself but can't seem to stop the desire for vengeance. Jaden tries to watch television and finds himself identifying with the bad guys in the psychodramas Michael and he used to enjoy together. Jaden thinks he now knows what it takes to tip ordinary people over into committing the most terrible acts of violence. Jaden imagines Michael dealing with his death. What if he had died instead of Michael. How would Michael be feeling? An idea begins to take root in his grief-soaked mind that it might have been better if he, Jaden had died and Michael had lived. Michael was a good person. He was kind and tried to help people. Jaden feels he has turned into something monstrous. He feels guilty for making such a terrible job of living when poor Michael didn't get that chance.

I want to convey to you the depth of despair that Jaden feels and the power of his rage. I want if I can to help you notice how these feelings are all-consuming. They aren't the kind of feelings that are going to change quickly. They can't be made to go away by focussing on the positives or remembering that there are always people worse off than oneself – these are pieces of advice often offered to the bereaved. Sometimes the bereaved person themself adds to their own misery – a bit like Jaden is doing – by feeling as if they have turned into a terrible person who barely deserves to live. These feelings of rage, guilt and shame, and of course the feelings that you may be going through right now as you read, require careful handling.

I have learned that pushing feelings down and trying to deny them is often not a helpful strategy. I'm not a medical doctor but I firmly believe that there are very strong connections between our emotions and our physical health. Feelings like these are unlikely to do anything but cause harm unless we can learn how to respond to them.

HOW CAN I LEARN TO DEAL WITH THE WORST OF MY FEELINGS?

So where to begin? We have already learned that rules in grief tend not to be helpful. We have discovered that grief is not predictable. Jaden not only feels what he feels about Michael's death and specifically about the man driving the car that killed Michael; he also feels guilty and ashamed. It can be useful to find an analogy that works for you to help you get to grips with some of your feelings and really envision what they are and what it's like to experience them. In therapy we might look for an analogy that works for you. I'm a keen domestic cook so pressure cookers needing to release steam, pots that boil over and fat that spits up in your face are all ideas that work for me. I have had clients who love the outdoors, in which case extreme weather conditions, mountains to climb and something called a false summit works for them. If you are curious, a false summit is when you think you have the measure of how much further there is to go and then realise there's a whole other, additional part of the journey you hadn't even realised was there. An idea that I think works well for understanding grief.

Can you think about what your grief is like for you? What images come to mind? Imagine if you were abducted by aliens who would only let you go once you had explained what your grief is like. What would you say if you were being forced to say something? Sometimes an abstract can work. What colour is your grief? If your grief were a piece of music, what would it sound like? The point of all this is that in order to learn to live with your grief you are going to need to get to know it. Listen to what it – and therefore you – need. Often feelings that go unexpressed and denied just carry on shouting a bit louder until they get the attention they require. Jaden feels highly cynical about all this. Before Michael died, he would have been quite open to these ideas but now he thinks they are a load of old psychobabble nonsense. Nonetheless he decides to give it a go even if it's just to prove to himself that nothing will help. Jaden imagines his grief like a powerful and destructive fire. He remembers learning about volcanoes at school when he was a child and doing a picture of one in his art class. He imagines how big the canvas would need to be and how much paint he would have to use recreate the feelings he has now. He sees himself throwing pain at an enormous wall mounted canvas. He remembers going to a gallery in Paris with Michael and looking at some huge paintings that to them looked a lot like someone had done just that. He remembers them laughing about it. He starts to cry. Eventually, once he is so exhausted that he can't cry any more he falls asleep.

I'm sorry to say that none of this is a magic spell that will make life easier for Jaden. At least not yet. But it is a start. A start that allows him to feel what he feels, find ways to imagine it and make some sense of it. It gave him a memory of a happier time with Michael that made him cry but was for a moment better than the all-consuming rage he had been feeling. Jaden has taken a step towards facing the worst of some of his feelings. He remembers that Michael would want him to find ways to live and be devastated at the state he finds himself in. Very tentatively Jaden feels the smallest amount of self-compassion glimmer within himself.

WHY DO I FEEL SO MANY DIFFERENT AND OFTEN COMPLETELY UNEXPECTED THINGS?

I have come to believe that one of the things that makes grief and living with loss so difficult is that it is an experience like no other in terms of how changeable it can be. With other less overwhelming feelings, I notice they have a kind of shelf life that I can get a sense of. If I feel irritated with somebody I care about the chances are the feeling won't last. It will either fade away or I might gain a different perspective and realise I too can be irritating (shocking I know). If I feel tired, I can look forward to getting some rest at the earliest opportunity. If I feel sad at the state of the world – and I do – I can try to focus on small acts of kindness or maybe some pleasant distraction for a while. In other words, I can do things about how I feel and I can to some extent at least, have an expectation about how things will go based on life experience and self-knowledge.

Now let's talk about grief … At this point I feel like I don't need to tell you that none of the above seems to apply when it comes to dealing with loss and feelings of grief. We have become acquainted with Jaden's rage already. What I haven't shared is that he feels all this terrible rage and at the same time, somehow, he finds ways to continue to live his life as best he can. He speaks to people and responds when they ask him how he is. He sometimes manages to eat. He has dealt with all the awful admin associated with a death. He has organised Michael's funeral. Reading this, you might imagine that his feelings can't be all that overwhelming if he is managing to do all this. But they are just as overwhelming as you might have imagined and I tried to convey AND he is somehow able to do at least some of the ordinary things of life. He has even managed the far less ordinary task of organising and attending his partner's funeral. I wonder if you recognise any of this strangeness in yourself. How one minute you can be trying to do something ordinary and the next you can be assaulted by a wave of grief that appears to come out of nowhere and leaves you gasping for breath and fearing you have lost control of your senses?

There is a theory about grief that I find helpful called the **Dual Processing Model**. It was developed by Dr Margaret Stroebe and Dr Henk Schut in 1999 and I think it goes some way to offering a way of understanding those sudden shifts in feelings that appear to have no discernible pattern to them and which can be so horribly alarming. The Dual Processing Model essentially does what you might it imagine it does when you think of its name. It suggests that broadly there are two things going on in grief. The first of which is what's called the Loss Orientation. This is the state in which you might find yourself feeling sadness; perhaps longing for the deceased; and noticing that grief intrudes into and takes over any other feelings. The second orientation is called Restoration Orientation. This is when you might find yourself temporarily distracted from your grief, having to do new or different things and just generally trying to get on with life the best you can.

Often the Dual Processing Model appears in the literature as two circles, one for each orientation: Loss and Restoration. I'd like to invite you to think of what you might include is each of your circles. Keep it simple. First, try to think of what you are doing and feeling when you are immersed in your grief. You might think of things like:

- Crying
- Staring into space
- Looking at a photograph of your person

These then are descriptors of how it is for you when you are in Loss orientation.

Now think of what you might include in the other circle. Your Restoration orientation. Some examples might be:

- Going food shopping
- Doing necessary domestic tasks
- Talking to people without breaking down

Dual processing suggests that we oscillate between these two states often quickly and without much warning and sometimes much more slowly. The thing with theories is they are always generalisations. I would like to add four of the lessons I have learned about how this model applies to real people dealing with and living with real loss.

Lesson 1

It's quite possible to feel guilty in either orientation if you haven't done the work on accepting that you are allowed to feel whatever you feel, whenever you feel it. Jaden feels guilty when he is in Loss orientation that Michael would want him to be getting on with life, that he is somehow failing to cope very well and letting Michael and his memory down. He feels just as guilty when he is Restoration Orientation. He can't believe he could find himself smiling, even for a moment, when Michael is not here to smile with him. The ordinary things of life seem pointless and meaningless and yet somehow Jaden finds himself buying milk, taking out the rubbish and putting one foot in front of the other.

Lesson 2

Sometimes there can be triggers that might send you into one orientation or the other. A knock at the door might place you in Restoration Orientation as you open the door, engage with the delivery person and try to act normally. An evocative scent that reminds you so painfully of the person you have lost might send you very quickly into Loss Orientation. Sometimes triggers are reasonably clear. Sometimes not. They can be hard to discern and may be generated in parts of yourself you are not even aware of. This can feel horribly confusing and make living life very unstable. People lose confidence to go out and face the world when at any moment they know they might be felled by their grief that can feel like it comes out of nowhere.

Lesson 3

The shifts from one set of feelings to another are what Stroebe and Schut call Oscillation and are themselves exhausting, bewildering and generally reinforce the feeling that you no longer have any control or say over what you feel, when you feel it or what is going to happen to you next. When you stop to think about that it can take you back to a very infantilised state. Even from really early on in a child's life the child will attempt to try to assert will over what happens to them and what they do. Now imagine that after years of having some say in how you feel and what you do, grief comes along and takes all that away. Is it any wonder that living with loss can make you feel like a helpless, vulnerable child at least some of the time?

Lesson 4

No theory ever gets close to a person's individual experience of grief and loss because, as I said when introducing you to these ideas, theories are generalisations. Grief and loss are personal to you. However, I have seen that people do find comfort in things that help them to make some sense of what can seem like the utterly incomprehensible and unpredictable business of grief. I think it's useful to take whatever you can and leave the rest for someone else. I hope you will take that approach to Dual Processing and indeed to everything I offer you here in this book. You decide what makes sense to you because one of the key tasks of grief is to make sense of your experiences in a way that is meaningful to you.

SOME OF MY THOUGHTS ARE VERY STRANGE. AM I LOSING GRIP ON MY OWN REALITY?

Some of the people I have worked with on grief over the years have been young children. Grief therapy with little children is as you might imagine a bit different from working with adults. Children are usually invited into a space that has things like a sand tray, model animals, puppets and a doll's house to help them play out their feelings. I have learned a great deal from grieving children, some of which I hope to share with you. I think there is much to be learned from children that may well be relevant to some of the stranger things you may find yourself thinking and feeling. When someone important to a child dies, they will try to make sense of it the best way they can. It is common for a child to repeatedly ask if someone is dead and whether they are coming back. The permanence of death is very difficult for them to comprehend and accept. Does this sound familiar at all? Most of us experience a sense of disbelief when someone dies. People will often say things like 'I can't believe I am never going to see her again' or 'I keep wondering where he's gone and half expecting him to walk back through the door like he used to'. Jaden feels like this about Michael. He just can't get his head around never seeing him again, never holding his hand, never feeling him breathing beside him in bed at night. He sometimes goes to get two mugs down from the cupboard when he switches the kettle on. Then the reality hits him again. Sometimes Jaden wishes his brain would just get on with understanding what has happened and other times he does everything he can to resist accepting he will never see Michael again.

One of the ways young children sometimes try to cope with the death of a loved one is to pretend they aren't really dead. They will tell themselves stories about where Dad has gone to and that soon he will be coming back. They might imagine that Grandma is on holiday rather than dead. From time to time grieving children might even tell other people these stories because if they can get others to believe it then it must be true and there is a kind of comfort in these mechanisms of denial. As you may be beginning to suspect, it's not just children who engage in this kind of thinking. I use them as an example because I think for most of us it is easier to understand and empathise with these imaginary children than it might be to be kind to ourselves if we find ourselves using any of these ways to cope. We are far more likely to think of ourselves as silly and stupid than an imaginary child. I am hoping that by imagining a child, struggling to come to terms with an awful loss the best they can, you might be able to extend some of that compassion to yourself or to others you are hoping to support. Grief is a wild, untamed emotion in my view, and it can make us feel and think some very odd things indeed. Joan Didion famously wrote a book about this called *The Year of Magical Thinking*. After her husband's death Joan found herself unable to accept the truth of what had happened and instead, amongst many things she shares in her wonderful book, she kept his shoes in case he returned.

HOW CAN I KEEP MYSELF SAFE?

I want to return to Jaden and explore a bit more about how some of these ideas are affecting him. After that we can have a think about how you can begin to recognise and respond to some of the stranger things you might be feeling. But before we do any of that let's start with some ways to keep yourself safe especially if you some of your more frightening thoughts have led you to wonder if life is worth carrying on with.

- Accept that you are likely to feel a lot of powerful, overwhelming and sometimes frightening things
- Learn to keep an eye on yourself. This is a process referred to by some psychotherapists as 'mentalising'. It means the capacity to notice and reflect on mental states such as thoughts, desires, emotions and attitudes. Some of the exercises I have already suggested you might want to try are based on the idea of growing your capacity to mentalise

your state of being. The idea being that the more we grow our capacity to notice and understand our feelings and so on, the more our capacity to survive and cope with them becomes
- Decide what you will do if things become unmanageable for you. In the UK the Samaritans have a very useful section on their website about creating a safety plan that is aimed at people who might be trying to deal with suicidal feelings and urges. I have included the details of this in the reference section or you can simply Google: The Samaritans, Safety Plan to find what I am talking about. This might be a controversial thing for me to say and I have certainly come across some very skilled therapists who believe working with someone experiencing suicidal thoughts is too much of a risk. My experience is different. I think that it is actually quite rare to find someone who is catastrophically bereaved who hasn't asked themselves if life is worth living
- Recognise that there is an enormous difference between thinking something and acting on something. It's not for me to make decisions for anyone else about how they conduct themselves both in life and death. I will say that my experience has taught me that it is possible to gradually grow meaning again after someone dies. To perhaps find a different kind of meaning and even happiness. It may not ever be the same as it was, how could it be? But nonetheless people do find reasons to continue to try to live with grief rather than choose the alternative. Part of keeping yourself safe is to hold on to the idea of this even if sometimes it feels very far away from where you find yourself right now

Jaden finds that one of the ways he keeps himself safe is by using his imagination, or as Joan Didion refers to it, his capacity for 'magical thinking'. He is not really aware he is doing this until his sister asks him, as they sit drinking coffee in his kitchen one day, what he is going to 'do' with all of Michael's things. Jaden has absolutely no intention of doing anything with any of Michael's things. To him they are an important way of holding on to Michael as much as he possibly can and keeping a sense of connection between them. The thought of anyone else touching things that belonged to Michael or wearing any of his clothes is unimaginable to him. After his sister has left, full of apologies for upsetting him and feeling dreadful herself, Jaden realises that a little part of him believes that Michael will come back. As he allows himself to notice these feelings, he feels embarrassed about what other people would think of him if they knew and scared in case he is losing his grip on reality.

Perhaps you can see, through this example of Jaden's struggle to keep himself safe and cope with his some of his stranger thoughts, that very little about grief is simple or straightforward. In one way Jaden is keeping himself safe by holding on to the idea that Michael might one day come back and need his things again. In another he is making himself feel frightened and ashamed by needing to believe this when he also knows it simply can't be true because Michael has died. These conflicting feelings are often a cause of worry and conflict for the bereaved and the people who care about them. Consequently, many bereaved people hide their feelings away because they seem so strange and confusing. The pain of loss has to co-exist with a sense of shame that what people feel is not OK and must not be shared for fear of judgment and other frightening and negative consequences. An important intention of this book is to reassure you that what you feel is OK and that adding to your pain with shame and guilt is an understandable but ultimately self-destructive thing to do when life is already tough enough as it is. This acceptance of what you are and what you feel is at the heart of grief therapy and is a way of being you can try to cultivate for yourself.

Jaden finds that where he locates Michael changes from moment to moment. For example, when he is out and about, perhaps doing his shopping in the supermarket, his mind locates Michael at home. He finds himself buying things that he knows Michael liked. One evening he cooks a spicy Thai dish that Michael definitely liked a lot more than Jaden does. As he sits at the table trying to eat the food he has prepared, with his face getting hotter and hotter and his stomach complaining that there are way too many chillies in the food for it to be comfortable for him to eat, the irony of his actions makes him smile and cry and then abandon the food. Later that night, he comes down to a dark, cold kitchen in the middle of the night to make tea and eat biscuits because he has woken up hungry. The loneliness of that solo act of self-comfort is extraordinarily painful.

At other times Jaden pretends that Michael is working away from home, which he sometimes used to. Jaden thinks back to how it felt to enjoy having the house to himself. To relish watching what he fancied on TV and eat food that Michael didn't care for – no more hot curries for example. He tries to recreate those feelings in the present, looking for ways to make his solitude more bearable. A part of him can remember the feelings and another part cannot escape the truth that this new reality is very different from an enjoyable break from one's partner before welcoming them home once more. The complexity of what we can now recognise as Dual Processing is that sometimes the two orientations, those of grief and restoration can be experienced together at the same time and separated by the thinnest of layers between them. Small wonder then that grieving is challenging to our sense of our own mental health.

WHY DO I FEEL SO GUILTY IF I EVER FEEL ANYTHING EXCEPT SAD?

Ask most grieving people if they feel guilty and it's quite likely they will say yes. As with most things about grief the reasons for this can be complicated and different for everybody. I want to share some examples that I have come across over the years in my work. I have created some fictional and composite examples to bring these ideas to life. I have called them: Recipes for Guilt.

- The woman whose partner died of a terminal illness who occasionally notices that she is glad her partner is no longer suffering or that she has to continue to witness their decline

- The child whose parent has now found a new partner that the child gets on really well with and who cooks better than their deceased parent ever could
- The man who still enjoys his hobbies and interests and finds himself laughing and enjoying himself in the company of friends before he wonders what on earth people will think of him
- The teenager who realises she still cares about her friends and wants to go out and have fun even if her surviving parent wants her to stay at home
- The mother who since her child died has gone on to have another child that she loves in a way she never dreamed would be possible again

I hope these examples will encourage you to notice your own feelings and get curious about any guilt you might be feelings. Sometimes the bottom line of guilt in grief is quite bluntly that you are alive and someone else has died. Sometimes it's more subtle and nuanced than that, as I hope my examples – and perhaps the ones you notice about yourself – will show you.

Jaden's friends and family tell him that it will be good for him to get out the house, to think about going back to work and to generally pick up the threads of his life. Some of this advice is offered with compassion, tact and sensitivity. Some less so but Jaden knows it is well intended. The now all too familiar mixture of contradictory feelings comes up for him when he thinks about these well-intentioned suggestions. Part of him yearns to have a break from his grief and immerse himself in things that will take his mind off the pain. Part of him wants to shut the front door and never talk to anyone ever again. If he can't have Michael, he literally can't summon the interest or motivation to do or care about anything or anyone else. Both of these feelings, and many others he experiences when he struggles to figure out quite how he is going to carry on living, leave him feeling horribly guilty.

I have evolved an understanding of the guilt experienced by the bereaved that puts it into two broad categories; Internal and Externally derived guilt. Let me try to explain what I mean:

Internal guilt

Many philosophers and therapeutic writers have things to say about the human capacity for what is sometimes referred to as one's internal moral compass. Put simply this is our personal set of beliefs and values regarding right and wrong. A self-determined code of conduct for living. It is not uncommon when someone dies to find that your internal moral compass is no longer as clear or reliable as it once was. Remember Jaden's rage for example. How night after night he lay in bed thinking about what he would like to do to the driver of the vehicle that killed Michel. Previously Jaden's personal code of conduct, and one that he shared with Michael, was to eschew violence and seek a peaceful solution wherever possible. He believed in these values as a way of living for himself and for the world he lives in. Many personal and political choices that he has made throughout his life reflect this. Now he finds himself feeling and thinking in ways that he finds morally reprehensible and guess what he feels about all of this? Of course, he feels guilty. And as we now know we rarely just feel one thing at a time so Jaden feels guilty and ashamed and confused and resentful. He also feels justified and defensive about his murderous thoughts. He feels like he has turned into the kind of person Michael would have walked away from.

External guilt

That last feeling of Jaden's, the one where he imagines Michael's disgust if he were to bear witness to the terrible things he finds himself thinking and feeling, leads us into the second form of guilt, namely external guilt. What I mean by this is the guilt that comes from imagining what other people might be thinking about us. Human beings are social creatures – even those of us who think of ourselves as introverted live in the world with other people and want to form connections with those around us. It's pretty normal to care about what other people think of us to some degree. It could be argued that genuinely not caring at all about what anyone thinks about you is a form of psychopathy. Equally, caring too much can be a dreadful burden on people's ability to develop self-acceptance and self-compassion. Finding some kind of balance that works for you is maybe the way to try to go with all this.

Now let's think about the impact of living with grief on one's sense of external guilt. Grievers often talk about how exposed they feel. How not knowing if you are going to be able to walk down the street, go to that meeting or have that conversation without breaking down in tears or storming off in a rage is horribly exposing. I remember the last time I was bereaved I felt as if my private feelings were somehow written all over me for everyone to see and even worse to judge. I couldn't look people in the eye in case they saw what I was feeling when I didn't want them to see or to form opinions about something that was just too raw to share.

Jaden tries to take the kindly advice of those that care about him and he gradually starts to pick up some of the pieces of his life. He starts going to his running club again and finds himself chatting and laughing with some of his fellow runners. Then he imagines what they must think of him. Do they think he can't really have cared very much about Michael if here he is seeming to be getting on with life? Conflicted feelings leap back into action for him. He wants people to know just how much he loved Michael and at the same time he doesn't want to share it because it's too painful and personal. He ends up not knowing what to think or feel except his old 'friend' guilt.

Perhaps guilt is an inevitable part of grief to some degree or other. I often say to the clients I work with that we will feel what we feel whether we want to or not and trying to repress, deny, shape or change feelings with brute force, coercion and control is probably not the best way to approach things. There is a good chance that what I have come to think of as the Rambo approach to emotions, trying to bludgeon them into changing or make them run off in terror, is not very effective. Who wants to get caught up in a way of being that is exhausting and unlikely to lead to much peace of mind?

Instead, I suggest that you get curious about what your feelings of guilt might be telling you. This requires that process of mentalization we talked about earlier. The one where you train yourself to take a step back from yourself and notice what is going on by reducing the intensity of the feeling enough to allow your thinking brain to start to help you understand what is going on for you.

Let's use Jaden as our example to find out what he feels guilty about, what that might be telling him and how he could respond to his feelings with compassion. Keep in mind how you might be able to do the same exercise with your own feelings

Jaden feels guilty that he can still enjoy things in his life and find things funny or pleasurable.

(a) He feels like this because he knows that Michael is no longer being given the opportunity to feel those things.
(b) He is concerned that other people will think he didn't care as much as he did and that he is a heartless person
(c) He feels that because he can enjoy things AND at the same time feel terribly sad, he is somehow faking his feelings and becoming a hypocrite

Jaden could try to respond differently to each of these aspects of his guilt. He could:

(a) Remind himself that he is not all powerful and he didn't choose for Michael to die. Quite the reverse, he wishes he were still alive.
(b) Find ways to tell other people a bit about his feelings. He could say 'I am learning to enjoy bits of life again but I miss him all the time. I think I always will'
(c) Give himself permission to feel lots of different and sometimes conflicting things at the same time and remind himself that this is completely normal.

IS IT OK TO SOMETIMES JUST FEEL NUMB?

This chapter has been about what I have called the dark side of grief. It reminds me a bit of when I was a child and my much more grown-up cousin showed me the album cover to Pink Floyd's *The Dark Side of the Moon*. I was a bit scared by the image and also fascinated. Now I think the music is pretty great and I notice I am interested in the dark side of our feelings. I have learned to understand them as part of what it is to be human. I don't think any of us can go through something as horrific as the death of someone we care about without feeling some dark things. I hope you can begin to offer yourself some acceptance of your more weird and potentially scary feelings. There is a difference between what we feel and what we do. You will notice that whilst Jaden has undoubtedly harboured some murderous thoughts towards the driver of the car that killed Michael, he hasn't actually gone out and done anything about these feelings.

But what if none of this seems to apply to you and instead what you feel is ... well ... nothing much?

I suspect most grief therapists will, like myself, have had the experience of the client who comes to see us saying they think there is something wrong with them, because they don't feel very much and they can't understand what is going on. I want to be clear here. I am not talking about those very early feelings of unreality and shock that I talked about in Chapter 1. I am talking about a more long-term sense of not feeling what your brain tells you you probably should be feeling, but you just don't.

The chances are that you may be responding to the trauma you have experienced because of the death of someone you care about. Trauma is a big, complicated psychological phenomenon and there are a lot of books written about it. I am not going to try to replicate them here but I don't think I can offer you my experiences of living with grief without talking a bit about the feeling of feeling nothing.

If you would like to learn more about trauma, I can recommend the best thing I have ever read on the subject (but of course I haven't read everything by any stretch of the imagination) and it is Steve Haines' book *Trauma Is Really Strange*. People get scared by the word trauma, perhaps rightly so, and fairly obviously it is not a pleasant experience. But I want to share that I have worked with lots of clients dealing with varying degrees of trauma and have personally experienced it myself. I have learned that in general, we can overcome trauma enough to be able to live a functional life.

Trauma is, as I have said, characterised by feeling cut off from yourself. People sometimes say they feel like they are outside their bodies, cut off and like a distant observer. This is different from the kind of healthy distance I have been talking about so far in this book. Healthy distance is where you step back from yourself enough to give yourself a bit of thinking and noticing space before returning to yourself and getting on with life. Feeling disconnected from yourself and unable to feel your feelings is much more extreme and sometimes referred to as dissociation.

It's not all bad news as feeling disconnected or dissociated is the brain's way of trying to limit and therefore protect us from what we feel. Unfortunately, it often leaves people surmising that there is something wrong with them because they don't feel what they think they should be feeling when it comes to grieving the death of someone close.

Contrary to what you might imagine, it is not necessary to go back over old ground, relive painful events or recall upsetting detail to try to deal with this. The brain is trying to protect you from doing just that because it has decided it is all just too much. You can allow yourself to trust that judgment and at the same time, gently and gradually practise noticing how your body feels right now in the face of intense sensations such as sadness and loss. The key words here are gradually and gently. The key idea is thinking about what is happening now, not in the past. Let's imagine Jaden finds himself feeling like this and comes to see me for some grief therapy. This is how I imagine part of our conversation might go:

Jaden: I just feel nothing. To begin with I was just furious all the time. Now there's just nothing. People ask me how I'm feeling and I don't know what to say to them. It's like I'm blank.

Sara: Like a blank screen on a computer … there's just … nothing there.

JADEN: Yeah. I mean I know I should be feeling things. God, I mean I loved the man so much. I can't imagine ever loving anyone like I loved him. I should be feeling everything but instead I just feel like … like I've died too I suppose.

SARA: Like a strange dead thing you don't recognise?

JADEN: Exactly. I mean I'm normally full of feelings. Michael used to say I feel ALL the feels, he …

(a long pause)

SARA: I'd like to try something with you. It's not about going back over the past. It's more about what might be going on right now. Is that OK?

JADEN: Yes, I suppose so. I mean it can't get any worse can it. I probably won't feel anything anyway.

SARA: Mmm that's always a possibility. OK, I'm just wondering what temperature your body feels right now. Are you cold, too hot, what do you notice?

JADEN: Well I haven't really thought about it to be honest. I suppose I thought I came here to talk about Michael. But I suppose I feel all right. Not particularly hot or cold.

SARA: You feel kind of normal temperature, is that right?

JADEN: Yeah, it's probably the only normal thing about me right now.

SARA: (nodding) So inside feels sort of normal …?

JADEN: Well normal-ish …

SARA: Tell me about the ish …

JADEN: (breathes deeply) Well the ish is probably the pain, isn't it. Only I can't feel it. Not really but I do know it's there.

SARA: You know it's there but right now you can't feel it, have I got that right?

JADEN: Yeah, I think so. It's definitely there.

SARA: Something is definitely there but you are kind of protected from it?

JADEN: (after a pause) Maybe … maybe it's just too bloody painful to feel right now …

SARA: Yes. It's just too painful. But it's there.

I hope you can see from this imaginary excerpt from my session with Jaden that gently and gradually we were working on helping Jaden to reconnect to some of his feelings in the here and now. In so doing he was able to begin to see that it's not that he is some dreadful robot man who feels nothing but instead he is a very sad man trying his best to protect himself from his pain to try to prevent it from completely overwhelming him. I also hope that you can imagine that for Jaden, there is some comfort in talking about what he thought was the deadness inside of him and realising he is not a terrible person after all. He is trying to look after himself.

I wonder what, if anything, you might recognise about your own responses to your loss from this imaginary exchange and from reading about some of these ideas about the dark side of grief.

Can you give yourself permission to notice your feelings as and when you feel able to? Can you recognise the peculiar contradictions of Dual Processing? Can you get curious about your guilt and how you might respond to it?

Can you try some of these things when you feel you have the strength to do so and allow yourself to begin to trust your own process?

GLOSSARY

Dual Processing Model developed by Stroebe and Schut, it describes an oscillation in grief between Loss orientation and Restoration orientation.

FURTHER RESOURCES

Megan Devine. 'Grief's Dirty Little Secret'. https://www.youtube.com/watch?v=IJ2tqUEKHIQ

Cariad Lloyd. On 'Grief Anger + Letting People off the Hook'. https://youtu.be/0xMA1cnOQoE?si=q-gXFo0PLGsJjoC2

REFERENCES

Didion, J. *The Year of Magical Thinking*, 2005, Knopf.

Haines, Steve. *Trauma Is Really Strange*, 2016, Singing Dragon/Jessica Kingsley.

Lewis, C. S. *A Grief Observed*, 1961, Faber and Faber.

Stroebe, M. and Schut, H. 'The Dual Process Model of Coping with Bereavement: Rationale and Description', 1999, *Death Studies*, 23(3), 197–224.

4

'YOU'RE NOT ON YOUR OWN' – HOW TO DEAL WITH OTHER PEOPLE

- What can I say to other people when they ask me how I am?
- How can I stop other people worrying about me and giving me unwanted advice?
- Social media is driving me to despair – what do I do?
- I don't want to get over my feelings – what does this mean for my future?
- Sharing your continued bond with other people
- Ways to keep memories alive

WHAT CAN I SAY TO OTHER PEOPLE WHEN THEY ASK ME HOW I AM?

'How are you?'
'Is there anything I can do?'

Are these the two most commonly asked things that bereaved people get asked? I don't really know. I do know that it is almost impossible to answer these questions honestly and fully when you are living with grief. Try it now. What would you say if you were to try to tell the unvarnished truth in response to either of these questions? Clients I have worked with have suggested some pretty lively responses when I have asked them this.

How am I?

'I am living in a nightmare. Half the time I'm not sure if I want to live or die quite frankly, but thanks for asking'.

'I have no idea how I am. My son has died. How am I supposed to be? How would you feel?'

'I'm currently faking my whole life. Nothing I say about how I am is true and I have no words to describe the reality of how I am even if I wanted to'.

'Is there anything I can do?'

'Unless you are a magician and can bring her back to me, no – there is nothing you can do'.

'I have absolutely no idea what I need, or feel or think right now. I can't even begin to imagine how to answer your question'.

'Nothing matters to me now. Whatever you do and however well intended you might be, it will mean absolutely nothing to me so you might as well not bother'.

'Yes. Just leave me alone. Much as I dread my own company I long for it because I find everyone else so bloody irritating!'

I wonder if any of these responses resonate with you. The chances are they might and I'm guessing it's equally likely that instead of saying any of them out loud you probably end up trying to say something polite like:

'Oh, not too bad considering' or 'No, I'm OK, I've got everything I need thank you'.

It may not be the first time in your life that you notice the gap between what you feel inside and what you say to other people. Most of us have learned sufficient social skills to find ways to make our internal thoughts and feelings acceptable to others and of course sometimes it's easy to do that. If I am feeling happy and relaxed and enjoying your company, when it comes to saying goodbye it's easy for me to say 'thank you I've had a lovely time'. I haven't got anything to hide and what I am feeling is positive and nice for the other person to hear. This is very rarely how it is when you are living with grief. I think this inevitable gap between what we feel and what we share and can find words for is part of what makes grief such a lonely experience for many people. You can be surrounded by people, or perhaps relatively isolated but either way when it is too hard, too complicated and often not socially acceptable to share the truth of oneself, the outcome is that we feel cut off from others and conscious of the gap between our own internal reality and the world we find ourselves living in.

So how can we begin to navigate the social aspects of living with grief? For me the first step is to accept that grief is personal, private and individual. This can come as a surprise to some people especially if you are grieving for someone whom others are also grieving. After all everyone is feelings things about the same person, surely there will be things that you have in common? The answer, as with most things in grief, is frustratingly contradictory. It can probably be best expressed by saying partly yes and partly a very definite no. Yes, there will be aspects of the person that will be collectively understood by more than one person. These kinds of things are often talked about at funerals. Someone's sense of humour, their love for music, their passion for football or ballroom dancing. Whatever it happens to be these are the more public and social aspects of a person that can be understood by more than one person. These parts can be very meaningful for the bereaved to focus on and talk about together, partly because it is a way for us to connect with each other in a common sense of loss.

The other part of the answer is a very definite no. This is because we grieve for the relationship we had with the deceased. Even if you were, often for complicated and painful reasons, estranged from the person who has died, your connection to them will be unique to you and them. No-one else can ever fully understand all that passes between one person and another. Thus, in grief only you will really understand and feel what you shared or perhaps wished you had shared and what you are feeling now as you learn to live with your loss. I believe it is helpful to be aware of your own expectations about grief and adjust them to acknowledge that some things can never be fully shared or understood by others. If you can notice when you feel hurt or angry or disappointed by how someone else is remembering the person who has died or talking about their feelings that seem very different to your own, you can save yourself a lot of unnecessary pain. Try reminding yourself that their view and their feelings will inevitably be different to those of your own. If you are able to work on the acceptance of this then there can be real joy in discovering different things about the deceased, things you may not have known or appreciated that meant something to someone else. I remember when a friend of mine died. After her death I learned that she had a long-standing connection with a charity I was about to do some work with. Part of me felt very sad that I hadn't known this when she was alive. Part of me was a bit relieved because my friend had a bossy side and I could imagine her trying to tell me how to do my work her way and not being sensitive to the differences between us. Part of me felt happy to somehow feel this continued connection with her after her death. Later on in this chapter I will talk a bit more about these kinds of continuing connections.

For now, let us return to the question of what to say when other people ask you how you are. I think it's useful to have a few stock answers ready for such a moment. You will know how grief can come barrelling out of apparently nowhere and leave you speechless and vulnerable. A few prepared answers can help you to feel a tiny bit more in control of things even if you never actually use them. But what should they be? My view is that it is helpful to include a grain of truth and at the same time accept that it is very tough and most likely not your choice to share all of what you feel. If you go down the completely fake route this can lead to an even greater sense of social isolation. It might put people off from asking after you again. Perhaps there is a part of you thinking that would be a welcome relief. However, we human beings are a contrary lot (although anyone who has ever loved a cat will confirm this contrariness is not exclusively human). Part of us yearns for care and attention and part of us can find it overwhelming and wish to push it away. At a time in one's life when it is quite likely we are feeling sad and lonely it might not be the wisest course of action to respond in an obviously fake way to a well-meant inquiry as to how we are. Even the most empathic person will find being offered something transparently inauthentic a bit off putting. So, a grain of truth can help you feel a bit less isolated and encourage other people to continue to seek out connection with you at whatever level it might be. Some good examples of the grain of truth approach are:

'I have good days and bad but I miss them all the time'.

'Trying my best to look after myself, some things are easier than others'.

'I still can't really take it in'.

'It's not easy. I try to find little things that help'.

And what about if people ask you if there is anything they can do? First of all, ask yourself this question. Accepting offers of help and asking for what you need is a skill. It means admitting to yourself and then to someone else that you can't actually do everything for yourself and that can be an uncomfortable reinforcement of the vulnerability of grief. Again, some pre-planning might be a good idea. Are there things you are struggling with? Do you want someone else to step in or show you how to do something for yourself? I have worked with many clients who have been bereaved after a long-standing relationship. In these circumstances it is probably inevitably that division of labour becomes habitual. There may be some things you need to do but you aren't really sure how to go about it. Think about the people you have in your life. Is there someone who could help you with something? Generally, people are quite relieved to be asked to help with something specific. Think about what these things might be and practise accepting offers of help in your head. Rehearsing responses is a good way to reduce social anxiety in grief. There is something about allowing ourselves to be looked after even just a tiny amount that can be surprisingly soothing when we are grieving, even if the thing itself seems relatively trivial. Let's face it, in grief nearly everything seems relatively trivial in comparison to the loss so we may as well work on accepting that.

HOW CAN I STOP OTHER PEOPLE WORRYING ABOUT ME AND GIVING ME UNWANTED ADVICE?

I have someone new for you to meet. Natasha, Tash as she is known, had a son Ryan who died. Ryan was 29 years old and the last time Tash saw him was 18 months ago. shortly after his 28th birthday. Ryan texted Tash and asked if he could come round to see her for his birthday. When Ryan left after his very short visit to his mother's house, he took with him his grandmother's engagement ring, a gold bracelet and a pair of diamond stud earrings. He managed to steal these items of jewellery whilst pretending to be in the loo. Tash knew he had been a long time and wondered what he had been doing upstairs but she simply didn't have the courage or energy to challenge him. She watched him walk off down the road from her front room window. She never saw him alive again. Ryan, as you may have been wondering, was addicted to heroin and had been for more than seven years when he died. Tash has no other children. Ryan's father had never been a part of their lives and Tash presently lives alone and works as a carer for an agency providing support to elderly people suffering with dementia.

Tash is not isolated. Although she lives alone, she has friends. Her mother died a few years back but her mother's younger sister, Tash's aunt, lives nearby and has two children of her own. Tash sees friends and family regularly. She has worked for the care agency for four years now and has made friends at work. She goes to a support group for people connected to those dealing with addiction. In short there are quite a lot of people in Tash's life who care about her. I imagine most of us would assume that to be a good thing. Dealing with the tragedy of the death of a child from such a horrific addiction is not something one would relish facing in any circumstances never mind if we were isolated and lonely. However, right now, a few short months after Ryan's death, Tash sometimes finds herself wishing everyone would just leave her alone. She feels guilty for feelings like that – as we know, guilt is the perennial companion to lots of emotions that people experience in grief. The reason Tash feels this guilt-inducing desire to reject and avoid the people in her life who care about her is that they all seem to have opinions that Tash finds very difficult to cope with. They have opinions about what she should and shouldn't be doing. Opinions about what she should feel. Opinions (lots of them) about Ryan and how he wasted his life, wasn't worth loving, took Tash for granted and so on and so on. When Tash took a month off work straight after Ryan's death some people were worried that she was doing the wrong thing. When she went back to work two friends asked her if it wasn't too soon and was she rushing things.

Perhaps in part because of the nature of Ryan's death, Tash feels judged for loving her child. She has no clear idea of how she is going to get through her life without him. She is simply doing her best every day to keep getting up, keep going to work and keep things as normal as she can. What else can she do? She doesn't want people to worry about her because it usually means that she is doing things and feeling things, that people somehow seem to disapprove of. Tash wonders if this is how Ryan felt. Everyone judging him and disapproving of the things he did and said. In some strange way that makes her feel closer to him. Tash appears to be absorbing a largely unspoken message from the world around her that she should stop feeling what she feels about her son.

This is not such an uncommon idea and certainly not one restricted to tragic deaths like the one suffered by poor Ryan. Embedded in our culture, certainly in the UK where I live, is the idea that death is something we should get over. Admittedly the timescale for this has become a little more generous in the 21st century. Perhaps there were good and sensible reasons for generations before us to feel obliged to get over death as quickly as they could. I imagine if you live through a world war there is an economic as well as emotional imperative to get over death quickly and get on with surviving and caring for our families and communities. In my lifetime (I was born in the 1960s) there has been a tremendous increase in awareness of emotional intelligence, mental health and the connections between mental and physical health and overall well-being. As a therapist, I feel this is a pretty good thing and something I owe my career to. But hidden beneath this veneer of new attitudes lurks a shadow of old beliefs, at least that's what I believe and have witnessed too frequently impacting the lives of clients I have worked with. Even when nothing is said out loud there are unspoken expectations about death and grief.

One of the unspoken rules of grief is that the power and intensity of our feelings will be determined by the nature of the relationship we had with the deceased. Seems fair enough on the face of it until you begin to consider relationships that don't fit the norm and what the rules might be then. Consider the following examples:

- The man who has a long and secret affair with an apparently heterosexual family man who dies. How should he feel?
- The daughter who is estranged from her mother by her own choice and discovers by chance that her mother has been dead for six months when she sends the care home some flowers for her mum even though she can't bear to see her (this second example is real and happened to me)
- And of course, our fictitious character Tash estranged from her son who seemed to choose drugs (or perhaps they chose him) over everything else in his life but whose mother loved him with a fierce and desperate love that is as strong in death as it ever was in life

When someone dies people will often say 'Oh I'm sorry. Were you close?' The unspoken implication is that we are really only allowed or expected to grieve if we were close in a conventional way. If not the expectations on our feelings are much more oppressive. I am not trying to imply that if you were close and your relationship with the deceased was healthy, loving and significant then your grief will somehow be less powerful. Not at all. I have worked with lots of people who have lost someone they adored in life and even then, one can fall foul of unhelpful rules about grief and the subtle implication that perhaps you were too close and your grief is somehow being made worse because you loved too much. I wonder if the bottom line is that societally we are uncomfortable in the face of extreme distress. Instead of owning that discomfort, we seek to shift responsibility onto the bereaved and manage to imply that this is their fault for feeling too much, or not enough, or for too long or some damn thing that explains away why people are feeling so much pain. It seems to me that sometimes we do everything except face up to the universal truth that death is inevitable, we are all going to die one day and it is a completely normal part of living relationally with others to be emotionally affected when someone dies.

What then might be some sensible ways to try to manage other people's feelings and behaviours around your grief? Believe or not I have often shared an ironic chuckle with clients about this double whammy of grief. You are the person in the eye of the storm, dealing with the pain of the loss and yet it is also you that has to find ways to manage other people's feelings and behaviours at a time when you are probably least well placed to do so. You may find yourself dealing with the worry and unwanted advice of others or in some cases the opposite end of this horrible spectrum. Namely the extraordinarily painful spectacle of realising people are doing everything they can to avoid you. This might be straight after the death or possibly once your grief is felt to be lasting a bit too long and is now considered to be something you should really start getting over.

The answer to these grim dilemmas lies in setting some emotional boundaries as best you can. People talk a lot about boundaries – at least in my world they do – but I think it's worth clarifying what I mean as they still seem a bit mysterious to me sometimes. Basically, a boundary is a way of defining what you are comfortable with and how you want to be treated. Perhaps I find them a bit mysterious as few things are ever completely fixed when it comes to boundary setting. What I find acceptable from one person might be substantially different from what would be OK with someone else. There are many variables even within the same relationship. The key is to start with working out what you feel comfortable with and what you want. There might be many reasons why this is unfamiliar to you or of course you might be really great at this in which case the people around you are lucky as it will mean that everyone knows where they stand and miscommunication becomes much less likely.

Once you have started to think about what is OK for you and how you want to be treated, the next challenge is to think about how you are going to communicate this to others. If you wait until one of your boundaries has been transgressed then you've probably left it a bit late. First, other people are not mind readers, and second, when our boundaries are transgressed it is highly likely that we will feel things – anger or hurt or some other negative feeling that will make it much harder to communicate effectively. Let's turn our minds back to Tash. One of the things that Tash is finding very difficult to deal with is other people telling her she is wrong to love her son. Tash knows better than most people, how Ryan behaved in life. He frequently lied to her, made false promises and stole from her. He broke her trust and destroyed the hopes and dreams she had for her son. Now he is dead Tash finds her love burns even brighter. Ryan is no longer alive to steal anything else from her and it somehow frees her to feel the love for her child more vividly. A very complicated and painful mixed blessing, but that's how it is for her. How might Tash set some boundaries about what she is comfortable with and how she wants people to treat her and talk to her now Ryan is dead?

When people speak ill of Ryan, saying that he was a waster, or that he treated her badly or some such thing, she could try saying:

'I know he did some dreadful things to me and to other people. But I loved him very much. Now he's dead I need people to understand that I'm just a mother grieving for her child and I want people to be kind to me about that'.

Boundary setting and communicating those boundaries is something people often struggle with, so let's try a couple more examples to help you think about your own boundaries and what you might say about them.

Imagine the person whose friends and family feel they are too sad, too often and should by now be getting back to 'normal' What could this person say?

'I know you care about me and I'm glad you do. My way of dealing with this is to let myself feel my feelings whatever they happen to be and right now I am sad. It really helps to be able to share that with you and have you listen to me. I love it when you just give me a hug and make me a cup of tea'.

What about the mother whose child died and has to deal with people telling her at least she is young enough to have another. Or her partner has died but it's OK because she can still go out and meet someone else. What could she say?

'I don't expect people to understand how I feel when I can't even explain it myself. It's helpful when people just let me talk. I like it when you do that'.

I hope this gives you some ideas about how to think about your boundaries and crucially give yourself permission to set them. You can do it gently. There is an old technique I used to teach called Broken Record which basically means you start gently and then, if necessary, increase the level of assertion bit by bit until hopefully the other person understands what you are trying to say. Clearly there are limits to this technique and you may need to bring a conversation to a close rather than allowing it to continue if someone really is determined not to respect the things you are saying. My experience with grief is that despite people being clumsy and scared of other people's pain they do generally want to do the right thing. So, if you can figure out what your boundaries are and a way to communicate them, most people will be grateful and listen.

SOCIAL MEDIA IS DRIVING ME TO DESPAIR – WHAT DO I DO?

Social media, and by this I am referring to platforms like Facebook and Instagram among others, is a relatively new phenomenon. Facebook came into being in 2004. During this period of time I have worked with many clients who have been hurt, angered and generally distressed by things they have seen on social media that other people have written about the people they are grieving for. Tasha is no exception. After Ryan died Tasha was able to contact Facebook and let them know he had died. His account became memorialized and to begin with she treasured looking at all the comments and memories his Facebook friends shared. Over time things became a lot less positive. There were negative remarks about his behaviour, his addiction and how he only had himself to blame for his own death. Tash took steps to change some of the privacy settings and manage content as best she could. As Ryan's mother she was also 'friends' with some of the people he had known in his life. There were comments on some of these accounts about Ryan that she found shocking, upsetting and impossible to ignore.

Other examples of distressing aspects of social media that I have come across include:

- Sharing things such as images and video clips of the deceased that someone is just not ready to be able to look at and perhaps feels that other people have no right to share
- Competitive grief, where people appear to be competing with each other as to who is the most hurt and was closest to the person who died
- Hostile posts, where people judge and blame each other with their version of specific events connected to the deceased

There is a strange and disinhibiting aspect to life online that can mean people either say things they would not be comfortable saying face to face or else they lose perspective about the possible impact of things that they post on other people. More unpleasantly, it can become a platform for grudges and grievances to surface and be acted out in ways that cause a lot of pain. It is worth bearing in mind that however you use and understand social media, it will differ from that of other age groups. What can seem quite innocuous to an older person unfamiliar with the subtleties and customs of a social media platform can be encoded as bullying and aggression from another generation who has grown up with these ways of communicating.

So, what can you do to protect yourself if you find yourself struggling with this aspect of loss?

I think the least helpful advice I have heard in relation to social media is to simply not look at it. If you have sufficient willpower to do this then that is clearly a sensible course of action. A lot of people may, however, find it hard to ignore. Tash found herself compelled to read all the awful and sometimes lovely things people said about her son. There was a period of time just after Ryan had died when she did little else but lie in bed and scroll endlessly through her phone reading everything, she could no matter what impact it had on her. Things I have come across that have helped to some degree are:

- Familiarise yourself (or if you can, find someone younger than you to help you) with how various platforms work and what if anything you may be able to do to manage things
- Accept that blocking and muting people wherever possible won't stop people saying whatever they want to but at least you won't have to see it
- When you are trying to rest, keep your phone somewhere you can't reach it without getting up out of bed or your chair

You will notice that none of these suggestions are even close to 100 per cent effective. Pain in grief comes in many forms. The vain hope that we can avoid it is a delusion. Some things, probably lots of things, will be very painful indeed. However, your view of the person you are grieving is your truth. Try as best you can to hold on to that and don't for a moment tell yourself that your distress over social media is somehow silly or that you shouldn't be feeling it. It is a part of modern day grieving for both good and ill. I like what Christianna Silva has to say about this in her article 'Grief Is Complicated. Especially when It's on Instagram'. She continues: 'Like all pieces of life that take the dangerous road from reality to social media, something shifts in how we feel, relate to, and examine our grief when we share it online. This can be good, bad and complicated – much like the process of grief itself'.

I DON'T WANT TO GET OVER MY FEELINGS. WHAT DOES THIS MEAN FOR MY FUTURE?

Wherever you are in your grief I would like to invite you now to consider a question I have mentioned before and it is this. If you could wave a magic wand of grief over your head right now that permanently took away all your pain but also took away every single memory of the person who has died, would you do it? In all but the most exceptional of circumstances I am guessing you would say no. That has certainly been the case whenever this question has come up in therapy. I had a really tough relationship with both my parents but I don't want to forget them. The relationships I had with them forms part of who I am. Equally I have, like many of you, lost people who I loved very much and those memories are so precious to me even as they cause me to re-experience the pain of my losses as well as the poignant pleasure of remembering.

A frequent fear that comes up in grief work is the fear that as a person gradually learns how to keep living without the person who has died, they will forget them. This painful dilemma can cause people to hold on to feelings of grief and sadness and be resistant to anything that might help them to function more comfortably in the here and now. I wonder if you can notice the presence in these feelings of what is sometimes referred to as black and white thinking. The idea that there are only ever two possible options in this case to remember and feel close to the person who has died with all the pain that entails or to reduce one's pain, learn to live with grief and forget all about them.

I also wonder if the phrase 'forget all about them' seemed blunt, tactless and a bit ridiculous to you? I hope it did. Not because my aim is to offend you but rather to reinforce the absurdity of any of us ever forgetting about those people we have had connections with who have died. We just aren't going to forget as long as we have the capacity to access our memories. Of course, there is a question of degree and for many of us it is very helpful to have things that help us to remember. At the end of this chapter there is a list of ways we can help ourselves to remember that you may find useful.

I would like to reassure you that learning to live with your grief will not mean that you forget. Grief theory has things to say about this that you may find helpful. Modern grief theory, specifically something called Continuing Bonds, suggests that we continue to have feelings about and connections with people long after they have died and what's more that is a legitimate, important and healthy way to manage our losses. The first significant work on this idea was published in 1996 by Klass, Silverman and Nickman in their book *Continuing Bonds: New Understandings of Grief*. Do you remember earlier in this chapter when I described how for Tash, Ryan's death means her love for him burns even brighter. How that is partly because he is no longer alive to steal anything else from her, and somehow frees her to love him more vividly. What Tash is doing is forming a concept of how she will continue to love Ryan for the rest of her life. His death allows her to move back from what was often a very difficult present reality of his struggle with addiction to remember all of him. She can recall when he was born, what he was like as a little boy and even, in a strange twist of love and loss combined with imagination, formulate an idea of the man she wished he could have been without the prison of his addiction. Tash finds herself talking in her head, and sometimes as she looks at pictures of Ryan to this healed and liberated version of her son. She finds it comforting and a bit alarming, as sometimes she worries that she is behaving rather oddly in forming a relationship with a version of her son that never actually existed in real life. If I was working with Tash in therapy, I would be looking for opportunities to reassure her that what she is doing is figuring out how she can carry on loving her son and be connected to him in ways that will help her to learn to live with her loss.

This is a gradual process and not one you can rush. Slowly over time, rather than forgetting you may find that you can recall more about your 'person' than the last section of their life. I sometimes say to clients that it can be useful to think of a camera lens that in the early days after a death is trained very closely on the recent past. These images fill the screen and don't allow for much else to come into view. Over time the camera pulls back and a wider view emerges. This can become part of what helps us to formulate a way of connecting with more than just the events around a death. Instead, we can connect with more. We learn to tolerate and treasure earlier memories and different aspects of what they were to us. We can, as Tash has done, bring that person into our present. This might sometimes become apparent to you if you ever find yourself asking your 'person' what they think, or what they would do or feel about something and knowing what their answer might be. These profoundly intimate ways of thinking about the people we care about who have died, can facilitate a continued connection with a new version of that person that somehow transcends the fact of their death. A continued bond will not of course, bring anyone back from the dead and if you find yourself thinking these ideas are all a bit woo woo for your taste, then fair enough. But I would urge you not to discount these ideas as figuring out ways to remember and connect can form a crucial part of learning to live with loss.

A continued bond can allow us to enjoy and celebrate parts of a person in ways that can also allow more difficult parts to recede. Tash chooses to imagine a version or Ryan free from his addiction that she can connect with. I have worked with many clients who over time can allow the suffering and evidence of ill health they may have witnessed in their loved ones to move into the background and happier, healthier and more comforting memories to emerge. The camera pulls back to reveal a wider and more tolerable set of memories. In this way rather than needing to get over your feelings you can gradually weave them into your present life in ways that are tolerable and tender.

HOW CAN YOU SHARE YOUR CONTINUE BOND WITH OTHER PEOPLE?

I hope this chapter is helping you to figure out the more social aspects of grief, what to say to people and how to handle advice, social media and so on. The idea of a continued bond can at first sight seem like something very private that you might not wish to share with other people and something that they may struggle to understand. However, I am not sure this is the case. Despite all the challenges of relationships, the mean things people can say in the disinhibited atmosphere of the internet and our own fears that if we share our feelings other people will think the worst of us, I remain optimistic. When it comes to managing loss and learning to live with grief, I believe most people welcome the opportunity to break the tension, offer comfort and avoid cruelty. Furthermore, I believe that bereaved people hone their ability to determine who is offering genuine compassion – even when it might be clumsily expressed and who is insincere. In my work as a Clinical Supervisor supporting therapists working with grief, I often find myself talking about how bereaved people seem to have an ability to spot insincerity at 50 paces. If this feels in any way true to you and your experience then I would encourage you to trust your judgment about who you share things with and go gently. If you tentatively share a memory or a thought you have had about the person who has died and it is not met with a response that makes you feel comfortable then pull back. Sometimes though, being prepared to take a risk and share something can result in some very comforting and life affirming conversations.

Tash knows that part of her grief is an overwhelming sense of shame about Ryan's addiction and a fear that people will judge her as a bad parent for his addiction and his failure to overcome it. But as time goes on and the camera in Tash's head pulls back and allows her to remember all that Ryan was and the man she believed he could have become her shame gets a bit less. When she comes across people who knew Ryan personally or knew about him and how he died she feels more inclined to acknowledge them. From time to time, she has conversations with people that allow her to learn new things about her son that please her. Slowly the world feels a little less hostile. She can sometimes share memories with people and one day is able to tell a close friend how she always hoped that Ryan would overcome his addiction and maybe even help other to do the same because when he was younger, before the drugs got hold of him, he was always helping other people. Her comments are met with kindness and understanding.

Your own experience of grief and loss will of course be very different from Tash. However, you may share with her the struggle to know what to say to people, how to react and what to expect in social situations. You may recognise the internal relationship, the continuing bond, she has built with her son that comforts her and allows her to live with her loss. You may even connect with her sense that she isn't sure how much of that is safe to share and with whom. Grieving people often have a very real fear that if people truly knew how they feel, what they find themselves doing and thinking they might think there was something drastically amiss with their mental health. What Tash discovers is that whilst there is undoubtedly truth in some of her fears and misgivings about people not everyone means her harm. Tash begins to realise that if she is to learn to live with her loss in a way that allows her to continue to connect with other people, she will have to be prepared to take a certain amount of risks. Risks means sharing some of the truth of herself with other people. The alternative is to shut herself away and become even lonelier and more isolated. Risks also means accepting that not everybody will react in the ways Tash wants them to. They will have their own views, opinions and feelings. They may without even meaning to, say things that are tactless and hurtful because it is impossible for anyone to get it right all of the time. Grief strips a layer from people that renders them vulnerable and easily hurt. Tash slowly learns to differentiate between people she really doesn't want to associate with and those people she trusts. Grief can make people lose faith in their judgments about others. Ironically one of the ways to rebuild faith in one's own judgment is to take risks and accept that sometimes you might get it wrong. Tash discovers, as I hope you will, that sharing memories, feelings and continuing bonds with others can reap some very positive rewards if we allow it to.

WAYS TO KEEP MEMORIES ALIVE

Let's start with the obvious ones – photographs, videos and voice recordings. Whilst these are obvious don't be surprised if you have to take this very slowly. One of the ways of determining how raw grief might be, is to notice what you can bear to look at or listen to. Things can change over time. What might be very important in early grief can change as grief becomes more familiar. Keep an open mind and remember the only way to do this is the way that suits you.

Less obvious things you might consider:

- Keeping an item of clothing in a zip lock bag to preserve the scent
- Writing out a list of key memories in a journal
- Creating a collage of meaningful images
- Creating a playlist of music
- Choosing a place where you can go to remember, this need not be (but could be) an obvious place such as a grave. It might be a place where you feel peaceful or somehow connected to the person you want to remember.
- Go on a memory walk. Choose a walk, for example at the beach, the countryside or the park (take tissues) As you walk allow yourself to remember different events and things about the person. Every time you recall something significant stop and pick up an object such as a stone or a leaf to take home as a symbol of that memory. You can make a note of the specific memory as you go – perhaps by using your phone, if you wish. You can go back and repeat the walk as often as feels right to you.

Ways to remember with other people if you want to:

- Host an event of some description where you come together to share memories
- Invite donations to a charity that would mean something to the person you are remembering

- Create an online 'memory jar' inviting people to share memories. There are various apps that can help you do this
- Invite other people to contribute to your music playlist

This is not an exhaustive list by any means and there are plenty of ideas online if you search. I want to conclude this chapter by saying that thinking about the more social aspects of grief, how to respond to people, sharing memories, disclosing feelings and so on is not something one can be proscriptive about. You have to find ways that work for you and that match with your personal needs for privacy and sociability. Therapeutically I believe it is really important not to shut ourselves away from the world too much when we grieve. It is natural in my view to draw in on oneself in times of profound distress. But I also believe we are – to some degree – social creatures and need to find ways to face the world again after someone dies. It can be a characteristic of grief to resist doing the things that might help us. When my beloved friend died in my thirties by taking her own life, I didn't think I could face making new friends. I was highly resistant. With the help and support of some very important people and my own courage I gradually realised I wanted and needed close friendships in my life and I would have to find ways to make that happen. Our fictional heroine Tash knows that nothing can ever replace the loss a child. But she learns that she can't hide herself away forever and that she has to find ways to very tentatively connect with other people and continue on with her life even if it will never be the same as when her son and her hope were both still alive.

There is a writer called Worden who talks about the tasks of grief and I think that is a useful way to think about living with loss. Worden suggests there are essentially four tasks that require our attention. They do not occur in any particular order. My own view is that these tasks are not things that can be ticked off a list because we complete them. Grief shifts and changes all the time and can loop back on itself so something you feel you may have attended to can recur in ways that can make you feel you are back at the beginning again. You aren't of course it's just that grief, like the continuing bonds we can build with our loved ones, doesn't end. Worden's tasks are as follows with my own additions in italics after each one

- To accept the reality of the loss – but don't freak out if there are always times when you still can't quite believe what has happened
- To process the pain – but don't expect it to ever completely go away
- To adjust to a world without the deceased – and understand that adjusting doesn't mean forgetting
- Find an enduring connection with the deceased – in a way that suits you

GLOSSARY

Continuing Bond Theory Developed by Klass, Silverman and Nickman, it suggests that bonds with a person who has died continue in a modified state from that which they were in life.

FURTHER RESOURCES

https://mashable.com/article/grief-death-social-media-instagram

REFERENCES

Klass, D., Silverman, P. R. and Nickman, S. *Continuing Bonds: New Understandings of Grief*, 1996, Taylor & Francis.

Worden, J. W. *Grief Counselling and Grief Therapy*, 1983, Springer.

5

MY GRIEF FEELS DIFFERENT TO OTHER PEOPLE'S – WHAT SHOULD I DO?

- Should I get help and what will happen if I do?
- I'm feeling things that I am really worried about
- My circumstances feel different to other people's
- How can I help myself?
- How to deal with painful truths
- What is the role of acceptance?

Up until now some of the key messages of this book have been about reassuring you there are no rules when it comes to grief. That you have to do grief your way and no one else's. I stand by that, but what if you are really very worried about your feelings? What if your circumstances mean that it seems impossible to share your feelings and that no-one else will understand? But things also feel complicated and impossible to manage by yourself? In this chapter I will introduce you to three new characters, each of whom, for different reasons have some very specific challenges that are connected to their grief. Three examples are not going to cover every eventuality but I hope that if you are feeling completely alone in your grief then these examples will give you things you may be able to relate to. I don't think these characters' stories make for easy reading. If you are in a situation where your grief seems in any way to be reflected in these examples, I imagine life must not only be painful as it for all grievers but complicated by things that can only serve to make things harder, not easier for you. The reason I can write about such things is because I have worked with people in similar and sometimes worse situations. I have watched those people struggle desperately towards a place where they can figure out how to keep on living with courage and grace. It can be done. I have seen it happen. Facing aspects of your truth no matter how painful is one of the first, most significant steps towards survival. Reading this chapter might be that first step for some of you. I am also going to talk to you about what happens if you decide to talk to a grief therapist, what you can expect and how it can help.

Let's begin by thinking about what is sometimes referred to as Prolonged Grief Disorder (PGD) I'm not big on these kinds of labels and lists. I feel a bit suspicious about seeking to pin down and define something as unpredictable and personal as grief. I'm also not sure what I think about describing grief as a disorder when to me it is a perfectly reasonable response to death. However, this has its place and has been carefully researched by people whose work I respect a great deal. I want to share these ideas here so you can make up your own mind. The following is taken from the International Classification of Diseases (ICD) used in the UK.

- Persistent longing for the deceased
- Persistent cognitive preoccupation with the deceased
- Intense emotional pain, such as anger, bitterness, or sorrow
- Difficulty reintegrating, such as problems engaging with friends or pursuing interests
- Emotional numbness
- Feeling that life is meaningless
- Intense loneliness

The ICD goes on to state that to be diagnosed with PGD, symptoms (as they call them) must occur frequently and last for at least 6–12 months.

I wonder what your first response to both the label and the list is? If you are reading through thinking yes, yes, yes to all seven indicators, does it mean you have a disorder? The honest answer is I don't know. It is impossible for me to know and understand the specific nuances of everybody who might be reading this book. As with most things particularly to do with mental health and wellbeing, there are few definitive and consistent answers. It would be irresponsible of me to suggest otherwise. So, what to do? If you are worried, you are advised to go and see your GP or medical practitioner and talk through your concerns. To me that is safe and responsible advice. I also want to add things for you to think about.

My own experience as a grief therapist is that lots of people who are bereaved will feel some or perhaps all of the things on the list at some point and may not feel particularly surprised by any of them. We have already talked about the idea of feeling numb and shocked; the power of strong emotions; and the challenges of living in the world and interacting with other people. In my view it is a question of how much you feel and for how long. Some people cut themselves little slack and expect to be up and functioning again after a death in a matter of weeks. Society itself has implied expectations about how long is too long to grieve and shouldn't we all start to move on in due course? You know your life and you know the truth of what you are feeling. This for me is the place to start in figuring out how you are doing and what you need to move forward. You are already engaged in that process because you have chosen to read all or some of this book. There are many ways for people to support themselves; talking to doctors and therapists is one option. What can you expect if you do decide to go down the therapist or counsellor route?

First, I use the terms therapist and counsellor fairly interchangeably. Our profession is unregulated so there are inconsistencies to contend with. Always check the qualifications of any professional helper. If you are a UK reader then you might want to consider some of the national charities who offer grief support. Cruse Bereavement Support, Child Bereavement UK and The Compassionate Friends are three I am aware of. Your local hospice might offer bereavement support. They are all different so the criteria for offering services will vary. Another option is to pay and work with a private practice therapist or counsellor such as myself. We can usually be found either by using a search engine or a directory such as the Counselling Directory or those attached to different professional bodies. I am a registered and accredited member of an organisation called The British Association for Counselling and Psychotherapy (BACP) for example, and there are others.

Different therapists work in different ways and it's useful to keep in mind what kind of approach you feel might suit you. Do you want homework and practical tools you can try to support yourself with? Do you want help to learn to recognise and manage feelings that are hard to talk about? Do you have an idea that things from your past are influencing how you are coping in the here and now? Whatever your preferences you should expect to meet with a professional (either face to face or online) who is respectful and listens carefully to you. Be guided by how you feel. We have talked already about how grief can make us question our own judgment but ultimately you have to learn to start to trust your instincts. Therapy is not always easy and your therapist is not there to become your new best friend. Instead, you should feel they are a safe pair of hands and are genuinely interested in finding about you.

I think one of the most useful ways to describe the benefits of therapy is to think of your therapist as a helpful mirror. They are there to listen and reflect back to you how you are feeling. Often by simply listening to how someone receives and understands what you are saying (and sometimes not saying) you can gain greater insight into yourself. This can help you to learn how best to manage what you are feeling. A skilled therapist might sometimes tilt the mirror gently one way or the other so you become aware of things about yourself you might have missed or struggle to express. A therapist experienced in working with grief should have some knowledge of modern-day theories and thinking about grief and be able to tailor that knowledge so that it becomes useful and relevant to you.

Working with a grief therapist will involve talking about all sorts of things, not just the feelings you have about the person who has died. Often those feelings are privately felt and privately expressed. Grief therapy is an option to help you manage your adaption to this new, and most often unwelcome reality. Everything changes and you may find yourself talking about all sorts of things you didn't expect to talk about. It is all useful if it is part of what you are feeling and thinking about in response to your loss, so please give yourself permission to talk about whatever you need to. Remember, therapy is an option that doesn't suit everybody. Reading this book is something you are already doing for yourself and may be sufficient to help you keep going.

I'M FEELING THINGS THAT I AM REALLY WORRIED ABOUT

My circumstances feel different to other people's

I want to talk about these two questions as a pair. First, though, I want to introduce you to our three final characters, each with a story to tell that leaves them feeling different from other people and worried they are doing something wrong.

Emi was in a relationship with Rahul for over 10 years before he sadly died of a heart attack. Rahul's wife and none of Emi's friends knew about the relationship and Emi now grieves entirely alone and unacknowledged. You may or may not have an immediate response to Emi's plight. Perhaps you feel that to engage in an illicit affair means you have to suffer the consequences. Perhaps you feel angry with Rahul for colluding in a relationship that leaves Emi so isolated as she continues to protect the secrecy they agreed on. Perhaps you feel something different or not very much at all. Part of what is extremely difficult about Emi's grief is that there is no public acknowledgement afforded to her. Emi feels ashamed and weak as well as heartbroken and bereft. Emi's shame about her own behaviour leads her to feel anxious and defensive about the judgments of others even though the only judgment she is receiving is from herself. To begin with Emi maintains a somewhat idealised version of Rahul. She thinks about how he always tried to protect his wife and children and look after them. She believes the love they felt for each other was something very special because their need for each other overrode any sense they had that they were doing something wrong. Emi remembers all the times they spent together that were so precious and transcended the everyday to always be magical times that only they knew about.

A few months after Rahul died Emi notices that she feels irritable a lot of the time. She has a job she has always enjoyed that involves working with colleagues she has cordial relationships with. Now Emi finds herself feeling intolerant, snappy and short tempered. One day at the supermarket checkout the customer ahead of her notices a milk carton is leaking. It takes quite a while for another assistant to be summoned, the leak to be cleaned up and a replacement carton fetched. Emi is on her way home with no particularly time pressure on her but she feels herself reaching boiling point. She drops her basket of groceries on the floor, swears and marches out of the shop. In the car she suddenly starts crying and really struggles to stop so she can drive home. The next day she rings in sick as she feels so exhausted she can barely get out of bed to make tea. Emi stays in bed for days sleeping and sometimes crying. She thinks about Rahul and starts to think how he had the best of both worlds, a loving wife and family and an eager and attentive mistress. She feels as if their relationship was conducted largely on his terms. She feels used and stupid as well as dreadfully lonely and sad. She wonders what the point of her life really is. She has no children of her own and only a few friends, none of whom know how her life has been for the last ten years. Emi has some very dark thoughts about whether it is worth carrying on with life.

Rather than getting into a long description of how Emi might gradually struggle forward with her life (which I very much hope she can do) I would like instead to look at some of the key components of her experience that make this such a difficult example of loss. Drawing out key components like this might make it easier for you to discern if any or all of these things apply to you and to what degree, even if your circumstances and story are completely different from Emi's. Please remember as you do so that we are working on the assumption that awareness is the first step to learning how to address and live with the most difficult aspects of life. So, view this with an open mind. Your circumstances might be different but there may be things that resonate nonetheless. They seem to me to include the following:

- Secrecy that leaves no opportunity for public acknowledgment or the support of friends and family
- Shame about aspects of one's behaviour when the deceased was still alive
- The need to idealise the deceased and minimise any harm and hurt they may have caused in life
- The realisation of one's own distortions which begin to crumble and reveal a more painful reality
- Feeling stupid and used as versions of reality shift
- Anger and fury
- Depression and despondency
- Questioning the meaning of one's own life

Now let's meet Anna. Anna is 23 and has not spoken to or seen her birth mother since she left home at 18 to work as a housekeeping assistant in a hotel, a job that provided accommodation at a time when she needed not only a job but a safe place to live. Anna's birth father has never been in her life. When Anna was 9 her mother met and subsequently married her stepfather, Tony. He began sexually abusing Anna just over year after he married her mother. It followed an intense period of grooming where Tony showed a lot of interest in Anna. He came to parent's evening with his wife, Anna's mum. He gave Anna lifts and was friendly with the parents of her friends. Tony was handy and interested in theatre so he helped out backstage at Anna's primary school with their Christmas productions. Tony was helpful and chatty and well-liked by everyone. He was also a very proficient and skilled sexual predator. Tony and Marie, Anna's mother, went on to have a child of their own, Millie, Anna's stepsister who is now 12. Anna's mother has, from time to time, sent messages to Anna that she has not replied to. Recently she got a message from Millie, the first she has ever received, telling her that her father Tony has died. He was fatally injured in a motorbike accident and subsequently died in hospital at the age of 46. Millie says that their mum would really like it if Anna would attend Tony's funeral.

Anna has never properly told anyone about what Tony did to her. She has sometimes hinted that all was not well at home but never explicitly disclosed her abuse. She has done well in her career and now manages the spa at a popular coastal hotel. Colleagues know not to ask Anna too much about herself as she doesn't share a great deal. Anna keeps her accommodation spotless and is always immaculately presented. There are things about herself that Anna keeps hidden. Her hands sometimes bleed because she washes them so often. Anna tells people she has eczema and wears protective gloves to work. Anna has a problematic relationship with food and sometimes binges and purges particularly if she feels under stress. Anna's teeth, even though she is young, are not in a very good state because of the acid produced when she makes herself sick.

Imagining Tony's death is a fantasy that has given Anna comfort over the years. She has pictured herself at his funeral making a dramatic speech to other mourners describing what he did to her. She has imagined her mother begging forgiveness and showering her with love and care. Anna now realises these fantasies are just that. The childish imaginings of a very damaged young girl who felt she had no-one to turn to. The truth is Anna was – perhaps unsurprisingly – a difficult teenager, prone to bouts of anger and risk-taking behaviour. As Anna has learned to bury the truth deeper and deeper, so her rage has turned in on itself. Her self-harming and well concealed behaviours have replaced anything that would draw attention to her.

Would you imagine that Anna would grieve for Tony in any recognisable way? In life he was abusive, manipulative and cruel. He set things up very carefully to make it virtually impossible for anyone to believe he was anything other than lovely, helpful and respectable. How might we characterise what Anna feels when she hears that Tony has died?

- She grieves for something she never had
- She grieves for the loss of a nurturing mother, who although still alive, in Anna's view failed to protect her
- She grieves for a version of herself she can remember from before Tony. A little girl who was very close to her mum and was excited for her future
- She grieves for who she is now. A young woman whose pain is hidden under a tightly controlled façade of control
- She grieves for the loss of a close relationship with her step-sister. She also feels desperately guilty for leaving Mille with her father. She has no way of knowing if Tony abused Mille as he did Anna, but she knows it was a real possibility
- She grieves for her future. Anna doesn't know if she will ever be able to properly enjoy love, sex and intimate relationships
- She grieves for a life lived without guilt and shame. She can't shake a sense of responsibility for what happened with Tony and all the times she just went limp and still when he abused her. Shouldn't she have fought him off?

Our third and final character is Ade. Ade's daughter Amani has died. Amani very sadly died by suicide and was found by her girlfriend Hetty when she came home from her nightshift at the local hospital. Amani took a significant overdose of fentanyl. She wrote notes to Hetty, her mother and to her father Ade. Ade's note simply said 'Dad, why couldn't you love me for who I am? I'm sorry to leave you but you already left me.'

In life Ade had struggled to come to terms with his daughter's sexuality. Amani had her first girlfriend when she was fourteen and Ade dismissed it as a phase she was going through. He felt guilty and he knew it wasn't the politically correct response for a father in the 21st century but he couldn't help himself. Ade remembered

Amani playing dress up when she was little. She would drape herself in fabrics and pretend she was a bride. She used to make Ade play the part of her groom. Ade remembers explaining to Amani that he couldn't marry her because she was his little girl and that one day she would find a man who deserved her love and then she could marry him instead. When Amani began identifying as a gay young woman Ade didn't take it seriously. The relationship between Ade and his daughter deteriorated as she got older. Amani would ignore house rules and come home at all hours, in various states of intoxication that both parents assumed was due to excessive alcohol. Amani was in fact experimenting with a wide range of non-proscription drugs as well as alcohol. Amani and Ade frequently clashed. Lissa, Ade's wife, was distraught and tried very hard to make and keep peace between them. What had once been a relationship that gave both Ade and Amani much joy, soured and became unbearably toxic. Amani met Hetty at a club and was immediately attracted to her. Hetty was fun and physically attractive. She also had a job as nurse and offered a mixture of safety and excitement that Amani found compelling. They moved in together and enjoyed a passionate and lively relationship to begin with. But Amani struggled with feeling rejected by her father and let down by her mother. Once the excitement of their early relationship wore off Amani would pick fights with Hetty and accuse her of being cold and more interested in her job than having fun. Hetty got used to Amani rushing out of pubs and clubs in a state of distress. She tried to manage the turbulent and unpredictable nature of Amani's moods. Tragically Hetty was heartbroken and yet not completely surprised when she came home one morning from her nightshift and found that Amani had died.

Ade's wife Lissa was naturally distraught. She was also furious with her husband. She blamed him for keeping her away from her daughter. Ade withdrew into himself even more than he already had whilst Lissa's grief was noisy and passionately expressed. Lissa accused him of being made of stone and having no heart. She stopped wanting to share a bed with her husband. Ade moved into the spare room and would try to go to sleep at night to the sounds of his wife crying and him feeling powerless to comfort her.

Ade would find it very hard to describe how he was feeling, but if he could here are some of the things he might notice about his grief:

- It is a grief that is wildly inconsistent. One minute it is about devastating loss, the next impotent rage
- In between bouts of overwhelming emotion are long periods of numbness and unreality
- It is a grief that is experienced internally with little or no sign of anything happening or being felt on the outside
- It is a grief that is inextricably tied up with feelings of guilt that Ade tries often unsuccessfully to defend himself against
- It is a grief that encourages strange obsessive behaviours – Ade for example becomes fanatical about financial security and focusses a lot of his energy on earning and managing money in order to achieve some sense of safety and control
- It is a grief that feels like a punishment that cannot be laid down and must be endured for the rest of his life

HOW CAN I HELP MYSELF IF I'M FEELING THINGS THAT I AM REALLY WORRIED ABOUT AND MY CIRCUMSTANCES FEEL DIFFERENT TO OTHER PEOPLE'S?

Our characters have encountered some painful and complicated situations and there may be things in each or all of the examples that you can relate to. Whether you can or you can't I think most people's loss contains pain and complexity. It is not my intention to set up some kind of pecking order of distress with these examples that find you wondering if your situation is better or worse than our fictitious friends. If something is painful and hard for you to deal with, that gives your situation and your feelings their own dignity and validity irrespective of what others are going through. In other words, you matter, your feelings matter and it is you who has begun to try to help yourself by reading this book.

The first thing you can do is what Philippa Perry in her book *How to Stay Sane* calls self-observation. As she says, this is 'Not just another form of self-absorbed navel gazing' (that would be self-obsession) but a way to develop more internal clarity and more self-awareness. I have spoken already about the benefits of knowing yourself in pursuit of learning how to manage your feelings better. When the going gets tough, and by that what I mean is when you really start to grapple with some of the most painful and complicated aspects of your loss, that's when self-awareness becomes one of your most powerful tools. By the way, if you find yourself feeling dismissive of these ideas and thinking anything along the lines of 'well it won't bring them back, will it?', no. You are quite right. The point is nothing will bring them back and this is why I am continuing to try to reinforce this for you in different ways. We are looking for the things you can do to help yourself reach an acceptance of that grim reality and find ways to continue with your life. We have to confront these things at some point if we are to learn to live with our losses. In terms of this book, now is the time.

DEALING WITH PAINFUL TRUTHS

When I think about lots of clients and how they responded to their bereavements I have an idea that at least some of the of the things they did and felt in response to their pain were because they felt their pain was outside of most people's awareness and that was hard to tolerate. Most of us have a need to feel understood and seen. I can remember being absolutely outraged when I was dealing with a bereavement by someone who asked me how I was at a point when my pain was particularly acute. 'How am I?' I thought to myself. 'How d'you think I am? Bloody awful is how I am. I barely know how I am managing to put one foot in front of the other. What d'you mean how am I? What a ridiculous question. People are so insensitive' Can you see anything a bit off about my response here? Maybe you can't. Maybe it's pretty much how you feel sometimes. I don't know. But the truth is all the person had done was ask me an ordinary question. They asked me how I was. Not a particularly insensitive question at all, just as ordinary one and most likely kindly meant.

Painful truth #1

A lot of people are not going to care as much about your loss as you do. It doesn't mean they don't care at all just not as much or certainly not in the same way you do. And it is unrealistic for you to expect anything else. Even if the whole world was able to recognise the extent of your pain and what you are going though it's still not going to change the reality that you are trying to learn to live with.

I know it helps to feel seen and understood. I have built a whole therapy career on the principle that offering people the opportunity to be properly heard by someone who truly wants to understand how it is for them, is somehow healing. I get it. But there are limits to anyone's understanding of someone else's world and in grief this is something we have to learn to accept. Or else every interaction and every possible relationship we can have either now or in the future will leave us feeling angry and disappointed.

Painful truth #2

Learning to live with loss takes effort and it's effort you have to make perhaps when you least feel like making an effort. I have noticed that if I get a cold or a fever it pays to take notice of my instinctive responses as to how to help myself. I seem to naturally want to stay hydrated, get rest and so on. Unfortunately, with grief and other kinds of emotional distress sometimes our instinctive responses are not necessarily always the best option for us. When I am hurt my first response is to withdraw, to sleep and to stop leaving my house. This can be helpful in the short term but perhaps not so helpful over a longer period of time. What I am trying to tell you is that painful truth #2 is what you will need to do things you don't feel like doing.

If you follow your instincts the risk is you end up not doing things (like making yourself get up and about, go outside for fresh air or talk to someone) that will help you manage you mood and regulate your emotions. I can't tell you how to incorporate this truth into your life as you have to be the one to make difficult judgments about when something is helping and when it isn't. However, a lot of the messages in this book are about learning to recognise the truth of how you are feeling and this will help you to make these calls.

Painful truth #3

Birthdays, anniversaries and significant dates are more significant to you than to others and it is almost certain that people will forget. This does not mean that they don't care. Here is a good example of how social media can be helpful. Nothing to do with loss but I am fairly sure I would forget to wish some people I like and care about a happy birthday if it wasn't for Facebook reminding me. So, it is with anniversaries of your loved ones death or their birthday. For most people once someone has died these significant dates die with them. As with painful truth #1 we have to learn to accept these differences between ourselves and other people or else spend a lot of time feeling hurt and angry. If you want people to remember then you may need to accept that you will have to remind them.

Painful truth #4

Memories will change over time and there isn't much you can do about it. Of course, we can find ways to remember and treasure our loved ones. Of course we will never forget they existed, lived in this world with us and meant whatever they meant to us. In this respect we never forget. But the nature of memory is that it does shift over time. This is not always a bad thing and can be very helpful in learning to live with loss. For many people early grief is characterised by being unable to look at particular pictures of their person, or see them on a video or hear their voice. It is simply unbearable because the wounds are too raw. Over time these same wounds slowly heal over and become scars we carry with us that allow us to access ways to remember that can become extraordinarily precious. If you try to freeze time you will also inevitably freeze yourself, with all its implications for the quality of your life.

WHAT PAINFUL TRUTHS DO EMI, ANNA AND ADE EACH FACE AS THEY TRY TO LEARN WITH LIVE WITH THEIR GRIEF?

Remember Emi? She had a secret 10-year relationship with Rahul before he died. What does she need to learn to live with?

That the characteristics of her grief – as with all grief – connect to the nature and qualities of the relationship that engendered it. Emi and Rahul loved in secret and Emi now grieves the same way.

If Emi wishes to break that secrecy, she has to accept the consequences and that may be hard for her to face, or something she does not wish to do.

Emi feels very angry with Rahul for leaving her in this situation, and she may need to find ways to express that anger without harming herself or other people. Emi also knows somewhere deep down that she is an adult and chose to get herself into this situation.

I think there are some things that Emi could do to help herself that don't involve making disclosures she may not wish to for fear of hurting other people. She could access support for her grief that doesn't involve going into the specifics of who or what she is grieving for. She could confide in a friend that she is going through a difficult time and doesn't want to talk about the details but would welcome someone to have a coffee with or go for a walk in the park. She could consciously widen her social circle and meet people who only know her now and with whom she can form new connections. She could gently learn to forgive herself, take responsibility for herself and try to find ways to grow some new meaning in her life.

How about Anna? Anna who grieves for a version of a parent she never had and is left with the legacy of being abused.

Anna will need to accept, the best she can, that life is not fair. It isn't fair or right that she suffered the way she did. But that is what she is left with to deal with and no-one else can do that painful, reparative work other than herself.

If Anna can gather her courage and her capacity to be kind to herself – which will almost certainly have been badly damaged by her abuser – she could start small with the most seemingly trivial acts of kindness to herself. Deciding to pay attention to how she feels in any given moment, perhaps when feelings are at their least overwhelming. Asking herself what she needs and doing her best to give that to herself. I know it doesn't sound like much in the face of all that has happened to Anna, but I have learned that you have to start somewhere. If you dismiss the small acts of kindness you can offer to yourself simply because they are too small then you never give yourself a chance to begin to trust your own ability to look after yourself. It is easy to mock simple things but sometimes giving yourself a hug (actually a really useful technique called Havening, check YouTube for how to do this) or making yourself a cup of tea can help.

From there Anna can start to cultivate an attitude of care towards herself and see where that leads her. My personal experience of struggling with some of these same issues in my own life is that all sorts of things help, from professional therapy to attention shifting distractions, and learning to accept that I can't change what has happened, and no one else will every fully understand what it feels like to be me and I can't expect them to.

Lastly what must Ade get to grips with? My experience of having a relationship of any kind with someone who dies by suicide is that you have to accept that in some way, you will be part of the story that led up to the person doing what they did. You might only be a small part, or not and I am absolutely not apportioning blame here. Ade might choose to hold on to the belief that his daughter's 'life style' was part of what contributed to her unhappiness and he had been right to condemn it and her. Or he could engage in what I imagine would be some very painful self-reflection to think about his part in Amani's unhappiness. Either way and whatever I or anyone else thinks about Ade, his behaviour and his choices, he will have to struggle to make some kind of sense of what has happened in order to come to terms with it to any degree.

Death by suicide brings its own appalling challenges and these are just some of them:

- Shock and trauma – present with all deaths but heightened in death by suicide
- The question of responsibility – that can cause people to feel overwhelming guilty, or anger and rage towards others
- Making sense of the unexplainable – generally human beings are programmed to try to survive so to take one's own life contradicts that and is very hard to comprehend
- Risk to self – the urge to die can be communicated to others and risk to self increases with exposure to a death by suicide
- Re-visiting the relationship – in a painful quest to make sense of what has happened, considering one's own part in it and repeatedly imagining all the different outcomes if only things had been different

WHAT IS THE ROLE OF ACCEPTANCE?

Before I talk about the role of acceptance, I would like to say something about what I think acceptance often gets mixed up with and can prove one of the biggest barriers to achieving it. Acceptance is not approval. Let's look at the differences because this is important.

Approval is the belief that something is good or OK or in line with your values and beliefs. If you approve of something it might mean there is something you like or want to go along with. It is highly unlikely that you are reading this book because you have experienced a bereavement you approve of. Even if the death has released someone you care for from further suffering it is not likely you would describe your feelings as approving of their death. It might be a relief of course, but in my experience, death is something we always struggle to come to terms with whatever the circumstances. The important word here is struggle.

You may recall that in Chapter 3 I talked about the Dual Processing Model. The idea that grief involves an oscillation between two modes, one is grief oriented, the other reparative. For most people that oscillation involves a struggle. A struggle to try to get on with life and a struggle to come to terms with what has happened and a struggle to process the feelings associated with the loss. It's never easy – but you know that.

The role of acceptance is key in our quest to learn to live with our grief. Remember this is not approval but something different. For me acceptance in grief is about acknowledging what has happened without trying to change or avoid the truth. Another way to put it might be to say it is about making peace with reality. I believe this is one of the hardest things to do for a number of reasons:

Mostly you are not trying to accept something that you are glad has happened. I have never won the lottery but try to imagine winning an amount that was large enough to be life changing. My guess is it would take you a while to get your head round this new reality. You might have to keep reminding yourself that something has happened that is probably going to make life different. There might be a part of you that is a little afraid of what the changes might mean for you. But overall, most of us probably see a big win like this as something we would feel excited about. So even though there would be a process to go through to reach an acceptance of our new reality it is something we would welcome.

Now let's turn our attention to the unwelcome death of a loved one. Even in the grimmest of circumstances when our loved one has been released from suffering, there will still inevitably be a part of us that struggles to immediately accept what has happened. We will find ourselves saying things like 'I can't believe she's finally gone' or 'I keep thinking I'm going to see him later'. In a lot of circumstances death will most certainly not be welcome. We will resist the truth because the truth is deeply painful and most unwelcome. I hope you have learned through reading this book so far that some of that early struggle is a very human attempt to protect ourselves from a new and painful reality and allow us to come to terms with it in smaller and slightly more manageable chunks. We protect ourselves in this way from being completely overcome by the truth by allowing only segments of truth to filter through the layers of shock that are there to look after us. If we get stuck at any point – as we saw when we looked at the definition of Prolonged Grief, then the process of acceptance stalls. Acceptance therefore is something we have to work at and allow to take its course despite our unwillingness to embrace it.

Why else can acceptance be so difficult to achieve? In Chapter 2 I talked about the rules of grief. You may find that you have some rules you are living by – without necessarily being aware that you are – that give you a time frame of when it is OK to finally allow yourself to accept what has happened. If this is hard for you to notice in yourself, try this exercise. You meet someone you knew years ago in the street. Someone you are not particular close to or know much about nowadays. They tell you that their partner of 40 years died last month. You offer your condolences. They tell you that actually they are OK and they have worked hard on accepting what has happened and are now focussing on trying to live with the loss and get on with life. You say your goodbyes and walk on.

What are you thinking about what you have just heard? Are you thinking about how quickly your acquaintance appears have 'got over' their loss? Are you wondering about what kind of relationship they must have had to be able to get on with life so soon? I know I am – from what I heard it's only been a month!

What this exercise reveals are that we have expectations about how long and how much we might expect to mourn our dead and what those timescales and levels of intensity might say about our relationship with them. This isn't unreasonable by any means. But it can become a stick to beat ourselves with if we set ourselves rules that don't match with our experience. If our rules don't allow us to thrive and grow to whatever extent is going to be achievable for us then we are at risk of making a very painful and difficult part of our lives even harder for ourselves. And make no mistake, it is we who will suffer most from our own unhelpful rules. So, by all means think about what is acceptable to you but make it something that is within your conscious awareness. This allows you to check in with yourself and ask yourself if your rules are working for you and if they are kind and supportive or outdated and inherited from other people.

The final barrier to acceptance that I want to talk about here is the idea that acceptance of a death implies forgetting about the person, giving up on them and signalling to ourselves and the world at large (or at least how we imagine the world at large might be judging us) that they didn't mean much to us after all and their death hasn't really affected us that much. You could ask why it might be important to worry about what other people think. We have already seen we are social creatures to some degree or other and most of us are influenced by how we imagine ourselves to be perceived by others and crave some level of approval from others. I know myself that when I sense someone disapproves of me it brings out a childlike response in me which is often to pretend, I don't care by talking 'big' but inside feeling horrible that someone has judged me. I know I'm not on my own with this kind of reaction.

Then of course there is the more internal fear of forgetting and letting go of someone if we accept, they are truly gone and not coming back. This takes us back to Chapter 4 where we learned things about Continuing Bonds. These bonds are the ways in which you will never forget and can learn to find new ways to relate to and connect with someone, or to put it more simply, to keep on loving them, for the rest of your life. You have to learn to trust yourself that love survives.

I hope I'm doing a good job of selling the idea of acceptance to you even if you don't feel entirely ready to embrace it. My belief is that day never fully comes and instead acceptance kind of creeps in on you, but bit by bit. I don't think it's linear. By this I mean that for most people the challenges of grief are not straightforward. It's more likely to be a case of two steps forward, three steps back. I like the analogy of a game of snakes and ladders. There are things you can do to help yourself climb up some ladders and there are definitely things that you can do and things that can happen to you that make you fall down a snake and have to start over again. The reason I want to convince you that acceptance is helpful even if it feels a long way off, is to prevent you fighting a battle you are never going to win. The truth is there is something bigger than us that we can't control and that will impact our lives whether we like it or not. Whatever your spiritual or religious beliefs may be, death is an incontrovertible truth of life.

GLOSSARY

Prolonged Grief Disorder A way to describe an intense grief response that persists for at least 6–12 months.

FURTHER RESOURCES

Edgar, Taylor. *Grieving an Abuser: Journal Prompts to Process the Death of Someone Who Wasn't Always Good to You*, 2021, Independently Published.

REFERENCES

Perry, Philippa. *How to Stay Sane*, 2012, Macmillan.

Sarner, Moya. 'Why we all need Sisu – the Finnish concept of action and creativity – in hard times'. *The Guardian*, 10 February 2025.

6

WHAT'S THE MEANING OF LIFE NOW?

- How can I find meaning and purpose in my life in the light of what's happened?
- Three small things to try today
- Two years on – how are our characters doing and what can we learn from them?
- Is it possible to find peace of mind again?

In this final chapter I am going to try to answer these questions, first by sharing some of my thoughts and ideas with you, and second by revisiting each of the characters that we have met through the passage of this book. I want to invite you to imagine it is two years on from when we first met each of them. I hope you will be curious to see how they are getting on. I also hope you will notice that we are not revisiting them after a month, or six months or even a year. I have chosen two years because I think that is a reasonable length of time for each of them to have begun the process of learning to live with their grief. This is a not a process that has an obvious end point and may be something that they, and you, need to engage in for the rest of your lives.

HOW CAN I FIND MEANING AND PURPOSE IN MY LIFE IN THE LIGHT OF WHAT'S HAPPENED?

The first thing to say about what feels like a very big and very important question is that you have to want to find some meaning and purpose in your life even if it's true that it will never be the same as before. You absolutely don't have to want to do this all the time and it's unlikely that you will. But you do have to want to do it enough to make the alternative, and by that, I mean taking the decision to end your own life, something you choose not to do. My experience of working with clients is that most bereaved people at least once and sometimes more often than that, seriously ask themselves the question of whether or not they can face carrying on with their lives. If this is you my suggestion is that instead of burying these thoughts and feelings under a blanket of shame and anxiety you could try turning gently to face them. I believe you are more likely to begin to grow some new meaning and purpose in your life if you allow yourself to face the truth of what you are feeling. The problem with repressing our feelings, perhaps when they frighten us or feel too painful to face is that we end up repressing everything. This is often what is happening when people feel like they themselves have turned into the walking dead, stumbling through life the best they can and not feeling much of anything except numbness and despair. When we repress difficult feelings, often because it feels like the only option in order to survive, we end up repressing everything. One of the key messages of this book which shows up in various ways in each of the chapters is that learning to live with grief requires you to gather the strength and motivation to let yourself feel your feelings. I hope it's some comfort to remember you don't have to be feeling these things all the time. Distraction (as long as it doesn't lead you into the treacherous waters of addiction to behaviours and habits that may harm you) is a good and welcome thing. By all means watch that movie over and over and again, stare at your phone if it helps you, choose your thing and give yourself a break. But don't check out of your life too much. Balance is key and most of us prefer to feel we have at least some control over what we are doing and when we are doing it. Consciously deciding to face your feelings when you feel you are up to it is perhaps preferable to them erupting and overwhelming you when it is least convenient. And believe me, this is what they are quite likely to do unless you pay attention to them.

In the last paragraph I referred to the idea of growing some new meaning and purpose in your life. The key concept here is that it is something you have to grow, consciously and by putting in effort. I wonder how this idea makes you feel? Do you notice any resistance within you? I certainly wouldn't blame you if you did. The idea that here is yet another thing that you are going to have to work at when you perhaps feel least like doing so is not particularly attractive, I agree. It is, however, true – at least in my view. Someone once said to me that if you want to grow a plant, it's not terribly helpful to keep wrenching it out of the pot and inspecting its roots every day, before stuffing it back into the pot and waiting impatiently for it to show signs of growth. It's a good analogy for post bereavement growth. People, like plants, take time to grow. They require the right growing conditions and these can be tricky to figure out and can change over time. You may find the whole idea of post bereavement growth a bit ludicrous and even disrespectful to the enormity of your loss. If this is you then I would like to ask you a question. Do you think that you will ever be the same again and return to the person you were before your person died? If the answer is no then that suggests that bereavement has changed you. Could it be true that in order to learn to live with loss you have to change and adapt to this new life even if you wish that wasn't the case? My point is that in order to survive and learn to live with loss we have to change, we have to grow and we have to adapt, and it these necessities that combine together to bring about post bereavement growth. Perhaps the very first step along the way to learning to live with loss is to accept this idea and become even just a little curious about how you might help yourself to support this growth.

THREE SMALL THINGS TO TRY TODAY

First, a question. How comfortable are you? Is there anything you can do to make yourself even the smallest bit more comfortable? Adjust your position, get a drink, put a jumper on? Imagine you were looking after yourself as one might look after somebody who has suffered an injury. They are now in recovery and it's your job to try to help them feel a bit better. What would you offer and can you offer this to yourself? Notice your response to this idea. If you think it's silly ask yourself if you would think the same if you were really were looking after someone else, probably not. Cast your mind back to the idea of growth. If you want to survive what has happened to you – and I very much hope you do – then why wouldn't you try to increase your own comfort even by the smallest increment? Listen to your inner voice. What's it saying? Maybe it's saying what a load of old nonsense this is and how all this is not going to make any difference to what's happened and it's certainly not bringing anyone back from the dead. You are right of course about the bringing people back part, I mean. But it is not true that small things don't matter when it comes to how we feel and function.

Next up try a breathing exercise. I like something called box breathing this is how to do it:

Inhale for a count of four, hold for a count of four, exhale for a count of four, and hold again for a count of four. Do this a few times and of course stop if it makes you feel dizzy or unwell. There is good science behind this simple activity of focussing on your breathing and slowing it down a little that has a positive impact on your nervous system. Rapid, shallow breathing is associated with anxiety and distress. Focussing on your breathing in this way helps your nervous system to shift from a stressed fight or flight mode to a more relaxed state. I often say to my clients that the nervous system is a bit of a dork. I mean this kindly of course. It's a dork (dictionary definition: a slang expression to imply something is a bit stupid) because it responds surprisingly well to simply feeling differently even when nothing much else has changed. It seems to me that anything that offers a bit of respite when you are experiencing the unrelenting tyranny of grief has got to be worth giving a go.

Finally — and there's a good chance you may already be doing this as it's often an instinctual urge — can you find a physical object that reminds you of your person and offers you comfort? Use your discernment as well as what might be available. Some things are too painful; others afford some measure of connectivity and comfort. I have worked with clients who tell me that it took them a long time to be able to listen to their loved one's voice or watch a live image of them such as you might find on a video recording. However, they could find a still photograph, or an object that had significant meaning that helped them to feel connected. In her beautiful book *The Heart-Shaped Tin*, Bee Wilson talks about the power of objects to help us keep a sense of those we miss in the room with us. She encourages us to find something to hold when the hand of our loved one has gone. Remember that taking time to let yourself feel your feelings rather than try to put them to one side too much and too often is a crucial part of what it takes to live with grief. Find your object, hold on to it and let yourself feel.

Those are just three of the most simple and accessible things I could think of to that might help you to feel a tiny bit better even just for a little while, perhaps release some feelings and ultimately contribute to your capacity to cope with what you have to cope with and learn to live with it. In other words, learn to help yourself grow. I find this idea from Moya Sarner helpful. She talks about something called Sisu — the Finnish concept of action and creativity in hard times. Moya tells us it is something more profound than resilience. It is the part of us that comes alive when we feel we have nothing left. My thought is start small, get more comfortable, breathe, remember your Continued Bond and allow yourself to believe you can get through this.

We have two more questions to consider in this chapter but before we do, I would like to reintroduce you to our cast of characters. Let's see how they are each getting on two years after their bereavements and what lessons they might offer.

DALIA'S STORY

We begin with Dalia whose partner Dan died suddenly of pancreatic cancer, leaving her alone with their two children. Their daughter Ayesha is now ten and her brother Aaron is seven. Dalia has focussed on the children and has often thought to herself that without them she would have found it much harder to keep going. Both children received some support at school for their bereavement. They have made memory boxes of things that help them feel connected to their father. Dalia had a useful conversation with the school counsellor who explained to her that often children grieve incrementally, dealing with manageable chunks of feeling as they feel able to. She told Dalia that as the children grow older, they may become more aware of the future they have lost with their dad and should Dalia ever want to form a new relationship with anyone, the children's feelings will need to be addressed with love and sensitivity.

Dalia feels very far away from forming any kind of new relationship. The thought of kissing someone else, being intimate with them and inviting them into the home she shared with Dan seems unimaginably disloyal to her. Just as the children have in some ways helped her to keep going, the very fact that they are the product of her relationship with their father keeps Dalia struggling to imagine new and different romantic connections. For now, she is resolved to be the best mum she can be and prioritise her children. Friends tell her she needs to think of herself and from time to time she does do things for herself. She has started swimming once a week when her work schedule and child care arrangements allow. The feeling of determinedly moving her body through the water and focussing on her breathing is soothing and she has developed a small but nonetheless comforting ritual of treating herself to a decent cup of coffee after her swim. The glowy feeling of being back in her clothes after the physical activity and enjoying a hot drink reminds her of being a child herself and feeling safe and nurtured. For now, it is enough.

WHAT CAN WE LEARN FROM DALIA?

- Finding things that continue to matter is helpful
- Putting her own needs to one side and not rushing herself to 'move on' or ' get over things' is what is right for her now and that is OK
- Caring for other living things can sometimes be a way to care for ourselves. This can include animals and plants as well as people
- Feeling a continued bond is not always straightforward and can include feelings of guilt and disloyalty as well as moments of love

GEORGE'S STORY

In Chapter 2 we met George. He was 76 when his wife Pat died. Grief took George by surprise. Of course, he knew that people feel things when a loved one dies but he and Pat were not given to talking about their feelings very much. They had a happy enough marriage and George respected Pat's ability to run the home. Their daughter Abbey was a bit of a closed book to George as Pat had usually done most of the talking when Abbey rang up to see how her parents were getting on. Consequently, George had been confronted with a series of practical challenges after Pat's death as he learned to look after himself in a way that left him feeling awkward and ashamed that he hadn't really acknowledged everything Pat did when she was alive. He also felt a private and to his mind rather foolish pride n himself when he cooked a tasty meal or cleaned the kitchen. George often spoke to Pat. Not directly, he didn't imagine she was still there with him but he found himself addressing her as if she were somewhere else, looking on as he did the shopping or changed the bed. George did his best, partly because he was imagining Pat, looking on and he didn't want to let her down. George spent a lot of time watching sport on the television and he enjoyed pottering about in the garden when he had the energy. He knew he was slowing down but felt lucky he still had reasonably good health. Abbey and he talked more than they had done in years. They agreed that Pat would have been pleased with them and that mattered to them both.

George's grief lessons

- George initially feels guilty, uncomfortable and uncertain about how to do grief. His focus on practical tasks helps him to deal with this uncertainty
- After such a long marriage the Continuing Bond between George and Pat is strong. Without realising what he is doing George develops a strong and different connection with Pat in death. To him she is a real and comforting presence which motivates him to take care of himself and their home
- Relationships change if a space opens up that was previously filled by the deceased. Sometimes this can be a positive shift such as the increased intimacy between George and his daughter.

JADEN'S STORY

Chapter 3 introduced us to Jaden whose partner Michael died in a motorcycle accident.

Early grief for Jaden was characterised by some very powerful and difficult feelings. Jaden was enraged and furious. He felt ashamed of his own feelings and jealous of people more fortunate than himself.

Unlike Dalia who found comfort in concentrating on her children or George who felt he had a good and long marriage to Pat, Jaden felt cheated of the future he thought he had with Michael. Two years on and Jaden has tried various ways to distract himself from his pain. He threw himself into his work and now earns more than he ever expected to. He can afford to have domestic help and has dabbled in hiring escorts to offer him some sexual release without the complications of a new relationship. Jaden feels like he has locked his vulnerability away and presents a face to the world that appears to be content and successful. More recently Jaden has experienced what might be described as emotional leakage. Several times at work he has lost his temper and behaved in ways that are professionally unacceptable. He quite often comes home from work on a Friday and slumps on the sofa pretty much all weekend, watching television and ordering take-out food. He feels like he drinks too much and his mood is often low. The gap between what Jaden presents to the world and how he feels inside is significant. Jaden is frightened that he can't keep on this way and the recent outbursts at work have made him think hard about what he should do.

The absence of the future Jaden expected to have with Michael is the hardest thing for him to deal with. Jaden has a conversation with his HR department at work and decides he might need to seek some professional help. He begins working with a grief counsellor. It is early days but Jaden likes the counsellor and it is a relief to be able to let out some of his ugliest and most painful feelings. Jaden notices that the counsellor seems to be really interested in Michael and what he was like. Jaden finds it helpful to look back and remember all the things they shared. Driving home from his last session Jaden noticed himself smiling at a memory of Michael doing his impression of Jaden in a grumpy mood. Just for a moment Jaden experiences a sense of having been fortunate to have known Michael rather than unfortunate to have lost him. He realises that both these things are true. He recognises that for the past two years he has primarily been focussing on his loss. The possibility of the smallest shift in attitude takes root in Jaden's mind. He drives on.

Jaden's grief lessons

- Grief has many companion emotions. For Jaden these are feelings of rage, anger and resentment
- One of the ways we cope with difficult feelings that we may be ashamed of or frightened by is to hide them away. This strategy tends to have a shelf life and eventually may cause us harm in the form of unexpected outbursts, lowered mood and depression
- Grief is not just about the past. Letting go of an imagined and predicted future can be extremely difficult. The sense of outrage

that life is not fair (which it definitely isn't) can bring out very stubborn and vulnerable parts of ourselves that don't respond well to rational thought
- Sometimes it is useful to seek some professional help. The idea that dragging it all up and going over things again will make things worse is, in my experience simply not true. A competent professional will help you decide what is and isn't helpful

TASH'S STORY

We first met Tash soon after her son Ryan died as a consequence of his addiction. In the early days of her grief Tash felt like a warrior, protecting her son from other people's judgment and ultimately trying to protect the space for her grief to be felt and expressed without having to justify it to other people. Tash felt lonely and found herself turning to a version of Ryan that hadn't existed in life for a long time or perhaps ever. Tash found herself creating and connecting to Ryan as she imagined he would have been if he hadn't become addicted to heroin. This Ryan was fit and well and doing well in life. Tash would talk to him and tell him how sad she felt at how things had turned out. She would say things to him like 'I felt I hardly knew you at the end. We were always so close when you were younger' She would ask this new version of Ryan why he had let things get so out of control and if she had been a bad mother to him. Dialogue like this with her imagined Ryan felt more real to Tash in those early months of grief than conversations she had with friends and family.

Now two years on, Tash has become involved in a charity that supports people trying to address their addiction. She has done some fund-raising activities for them and has been trained to work on their helpline which she does one evening a week. This work gives her a lot of satisfaction and helps alleviate some of the guilt she feels for failing to save her son from himself. At the charity Tash has met Sonya and they have been out on a few dates. This is a new expression of sexuality for Tash and she is not sure where it will go. What she knows is Sonya is kind and funny and doesn't judge Tash for loving

Ryan in life or in death. The healed, imaginary version of Ryan is the version that Tash has formed a continuing bond with. Sometimes she thinks it's a bit strange but it helps her to move past some of the imagined scenes of what Ryan's life must have been like for him that used to haunt and torment her. Tash expects to feel sad about Ryan for the rest of her life and doesn't try to make those feelings go away. She will always be his mother and she is trying to be a better one in death than she judged herself to be when her son was alive.

Tash's grief lessons

- Forming a continued bond with your person gives you the freedom to decide who it is you connect with. You might connect with a younger version of a partner or parent, or like Tash create a version of the person that is different and easier to connect with than the one you knew in real life. All of this is OK, and giving yourself permission to do what is right for you will help you find what you need
- Learning to accept how you feel rather than fighting it and wishing it would go away makes life easier. The actor Alan Alda, now in his eighties and living with Parkinson's disease, talks about how living with reality is easier than wishing for what you can't have. This sounds like wisdom worth listening to in my view
- Finding some meaning in the life you actually have (as opposed to the life you wish you had or used to have) is possible and desirable. We all need reasons to keep going; even sometimes thinking about things other than yourself can be a welcome relief

EMI'S STORY

In Chapter 5 we met three people, each of whom felt their experience of grief to be unusual. The first of these was Emi. Her grief was something she felt she couldn't share and so she chose to contain it within herself the best she could. This strategy began to go wrong for Emi when she experienced unexpected and uncharacteristic outbursts of feeling, sometimes rage, sometimes sadness and often triggered by things that seemed completely disconnected from her grief for Rahul. Partly due to some pressure from work Emi began seeing a therapist. Her first goal was to learn some techniques for managing her feelings. Emi was disappointed to discover that there were no life hacks that were going to magically take her pain away. Instead, over a number of months Emi gradually learned to feel her feelings rather than try to ignore them or fix them. Emi's therapy became about much more than the death of Rahul. She began to understand things about herself and about why she was attracted to unavailable partners. Emi began the slow process of understanding herself better. She still missed Rahul but looked back at their relationship and understood she was becoming a different version of herself from the woman who had loved him as she did.

Emi's grief lessons

- Feelings require time, attention and acknowledgment before they can evolve and shift. If we try to deny our feelings, they have a way of surfacing up despite our attempts to keep them buried
- Sometimes emotional growth emerges from difficult and painful life events that cause us to stop and become aware of patterns of behaviour that were previously outside of what we knew and understood about ourselves. Awareness, whilst painful, can be the first step towards making changes to the way we relate to ourselves and others

ANNA'S STORY

Anna had been the victim of child sexual abuse that she had never disclosed. Now her abuser has died and Anna must decide what she does next. Anna has built a life for herself that is as safe as she can make it and she is very reluctant, frightened even when she really thinks about it, to do anything that might disrupt her precious sense of safety and security. At the same time Anna knows that she has her own private struggles that she tries to keep hidden from others and even a little bit from herself. Anna has read a lot about surviving childhood sexual abuse and knows that most likely, one day she will need to talk to someone but she finds she is not ready to do that yet. Her fantasies of going to Tony's funeral and making a speech stay as fantasies. Anna doesn't go, instead she goes to work.

After a year or so Anna decides to reach out to her stepsister Mille via social media. They have a sporadic and rather tentative series of contacts, liking each other's posts. Anna begins to think about her mum but whenever she does, she notices that her feelings are very confused. She chooses to leave things as they are for now. Anna doesn't grieve for Tony but she does find herself grieving for a life she never had, a life where she felt loved and safe and listened to. His death helps her to feel a little safer in the world but it also reinforces for her how alone she is. There are no easy answers for Anna.

Anna's grief lessons

- Feeling safe is sometimes the most important thing. Much emotional growth can come from connecting with others, talking things through, facing feelings and all the other things that I and most therapists advocate. But readiness is also a vital component of growth. Anna is not yet ready to disrupt her life any further. I hope one day she will feel differently but for now the biggest lesson that Anna can teach us is to take our time
- Grief can be an expression of the things we didn't have, the relationships that were missing or that didn't offer us what we needed. It simply isn't true to say you can't miss what you never had. My experience is you most certainly can and you probably need to in order to help yourself live with these kinds of complicated losses

ADE'S STORY

Two years on from the tragic death of his daughter, Ade is a changed man. He has been forced to confront his own part in the breakdown of his relationship with Amani. Lissa, Ade's wife, demanded that he do so. There was a point where it seemed as if their marriage wouldn't survive the death of their child. But it turned out that despite the appalling and continued grief they both feel for their daughter, neither of them wanted to give up on each other. Ade and Lissa have been learning to talk to each other. It is not always easy but they are willing to keep trying. One of the things that has helped is getting to know Hetty, the young woman Amani was living with when she died. They don't see her very often but occasional contact has helped Ade to realise his own prejudices and attitudes and how they contributed to the breakdown of his relationship with Amani. Their lives are very far from a fairy tale ending, blighted as they are with the continued pain of Amani's death. Ade knows he will die regretting his own part in what happened and often imagines the many ways in which things could have turned out differently. He knows that the man he is becoming is far more equipped to be a loving parent to his daughter than the man he was when she was alive. His growth is inextricably connected to his sadness and he recognises that will never change and he must learn to live with it.

Ade's grief lessons

- Some growth comes from the most dreadful pain. The growth doesn't make the pain disappear. It happens in spite of the pain and because of it. For Ade understanding and accepting this has been a process of becoming a gentler and more humble human being
- Acceptance of loss requires us to accept that despite the power of our feelings, they in themselves cannot change the truth of death. The only things we can perhaps have a chance at changing is ourselves

So, we come to our final question:

IS IT POSSIBLE TO FIND PEACE OF MIND AGAIN?

Having caught up with our cast of imaginary characters I wonder if there are any aspects of their different experiences and the things they have learned that resonate with you?

It's a classic therapist's technique to answer a question with a question because the conclusions you draw for yourself based on your own life experience are always going to be more powerful than anything you can read in a book, or hear second hand from someone else who isn't living your life.

I am struck by the differences in people's experience of love, loss and grief. So much is dependent on who you are, how you were connected (or not) to the person who has died, what kind of life you lead and how you respond to your own feelings. So, I want to encourage you to look at the various grief lessons of our characters and consider if any version of them might apply to yourself.

Maybe a useful starting point would be to think about what peace of mind might mean to you? I remember back in the 1980s when I was teaching business skills (about which I knew very little) in a polytechnic, I read about the good enough manager. Someone who does what needs to be done and doesn't waste time aiming for perfection. Someone who figures out the bottom line of what actually matters. This is a concept that also crops up in parenting literature. The idea of the good enough parent is that making mistakes is normal, and being OK with that makes you a more loving and connected parent than trying to set a standard of perfection and expecting your children to try to live up to this unattainable standard. So how about the good enough griever? What would their philosophy be like? Would the idea of letting go of doing everything perfectly and figuring out what you need and how you can best learn to live with your loss be more likely to afford you some peace of mind? I notice that two years on from their bereavements none of our grievers seem particularly caught up in achieving standards of perfection. They are all more concerned with trying to get on and live with their feelings as best they can.

Perhaps this less self-conscious state of mind has developed over the two years our grievers have been living with loss. When someone first dies it is our memory of their earthly being that is present in our hearts and minds. That's what we miss, the physical reality of the other person living alongside of us in one way or another. Earthly life is jam packed full of judgments in my view. Am I smart enough, kind enough, rich enough, thin enough? Choose your thing but my guess is it won't be hard to find some standard or other that has caused you to wonder if you are doing well enough when you measure yourself against it. There's no reason to suspect we would be any different with grief. So perhaps early grief is characterised by being caught up in the memory of the other person as they were in life and crucially, how they and indeed everyone else still living on earth might judge us using earthly (and often highly critical) criteria. After a while though our relationship with those that have died changes. I hope you are now confident with the idea of Continuing Bonds that allow you to keep on feeling things about your person for as long as you need to and perhaps for the rest of your life. Could it be true to say that the bond we form with our person after they have died is free from so much earthly judgement? I don't see any of our characters worrying much about getting a good grief grade. Perhaps the enormity of living with loss means that these initial concerns slip away and become less important. Could there be some peace of mind to be found in the idea that we don't have to perform our grief for a panel of judges armed with scoring paddles? Instead, we have to learn, very slowly, to just do it as well as we need to in order to survive. To be a good enough griever.

The final model of grief that I would like to introduce you, developed by Lois Tonkin, talks about the whole idea of post bereavement growth. Tonkin was a grief counsellor who developed her theory whilst working with a woman whose child had died. The woman explained that in the early stages of loss her grief consumed her and there was little or no room for anything else except the horror of her child's death. Over time the woman realised that her grief had not lessened but somehow, gradually she had learned to live with it and grow around it. Some days she would experience it as sharply as she ever had and some days, or perhaps even moments she was able to live her life around the grief. I came across Tonkin's theory when I went to a workshop about grief when I first started working in hospices. The trainer had a yellow sponge; the kind of thing you might clean a car with if you were that way inclined. Along with the sponge she had three clear glass cylinders. I actually think they were small, medium and large flower vases. She illustrated Tonkin's idea of early grief by putting the sponge into the smallest vase. It was quite a tight fit and there was no room for anything else. This, she said is how Tonkin understood early grief to be. It takes up all the space. Next, she removed the sponge from the little vase and placed it in the medium one. There was a bit more room now, so the sponge didn't quite take up all the space. Finally, she placed the sponge in the largest vase where it had quite a lot of room to roll about and only took up a small proportion of the total volume of the vase. The point she said, is that the sponge, representing our grief, stays the same size. It is the container that gets bigger. We are the container. Our grief becomes part of who we are but we can continue to grow around our grief so that our experience of living with loss changes. If we can accept that Tonkin was on to something, and personally I think she was, then peace of mind might be achievable by accepting that although your grief is not going to go away, you can grow around it. Might that take some pressure off?

My belief is if we can learn to accept that experiencing loss has a permanent and irreversible impact on us, we can stop wasting emotional resources on trying to make it go away when in fact it's here to stay. There is a passage in Andrea Oskis' book *The Kitchen Shrink* where she describes meeting Colin Murray Parkes, a very distinguished writer on grief who I mentioned to you in Chapter 1. The two of them share a pub lunch where Parkes explains that the stages of grief were never intended to be used as a rigid blueprint for what grief is like. I think it's fascinating that this is what they rather unfortunately became for so many people. I think one of the reasons for this is that the experience of loss makes many of us look for ways to make the pain go away. When that doesn't work do we cling on to ideas that seem to make grief predictable and finite? Makes sense, doesn't it? Except of course it doesn't really work like that when it comes to grief. The much less palatable truth about grief in my experience is that there is no predictable time line, no neat and tidy order and often no end. It just is what it is and you are stuck with it. Tough talk and certainly not as attractive as the idea of grief as some kind of illness that we can recover from if we just rest and drink enough tea. Could peace of mind come from an understanding that we have to stop fighting and trying to shape our grief into what we want it to be?

I love what Andria Wilson writes about in her chapter 'The Grief Dance' that appears in a text book I use in my own work called *New Techniques of Grief Therapy, Bereavement and Beyond*. She talks about how choosing an attitude of acceptance can help us develop a healthier relationship with loss and make the space to move forward. Andria says she holds the belief that 'meaning can be created from hard things'. It seems to me there is a lot of evidence that this might be true. When I stop and think of my own life, I can see that I have grown and learned from the hard things. I wonder if that resonates with you? It is hard to see what is happening for us when it is actually happening and we are immersed in the experience. One of the many benefits of working with a therapist is that it affords what Philippa Perry calls the art of self-observation that I talked about in Chapter 5. There is no reason why we can't learn to do this outside of the therapy space too. In a way the whole of this book has been an invitation to you to stop and notice what is going on for you and what you make of it all rather than just be submerged in the murky and painful waters of grief and loss. What do you notice when you stop and come up for air? Could there be some peace of mind to be had from recognising you can learn from the hard things of life?

To summarise then. I believe it is possible to find peace of mind after a bereavement. What you can't do is turn the clock back, have what you used to have, resurrect your person back to this earthly plane or change anything you did in the past to make the present different. These are the things you cannot do, none of us can, and you will not achieve much peace of mind until you can accept them as true.

What you can do is consider the possibility of learning to grow around your grief. The chances are you are already doing this without consciously thinking too much about it, because learning and growing are crucial components of adaption and survival, and that is what you are doing, right now, this minute; no matter what you feel or how hard it is, you are doing it. I hope you now know that surviving is not an indicator of lack of love or care or impact. You know the popular tropes about love, about how people won't survive without their loved one and that this is a marker of the depth and power of feeling they have one for another. I just don't think that's true. The vast majority of people find ways to survive the death of a loved one. It can't be true that all of us survivors don't really understand what true love is all about, now can it? I believe that every day you find ways to carry on; to keep breathing in and out and trying to do what you need to do to survive is a triumph of finding meaning in hard things. The decision to live is a brave decision in my view and testament to things we maybe can't fully ever understand about what it is to be alive and want to stay alive. Let's just celebrate it instead. I choose my celebrations to be quiet ones, mostly just me and perhaps a cat and a cup of tea but by all means find your own ways to celebrate your courage and allow yourself to notice it, really notice it and tell yourself you are doing OK.

GLOSSARY

Tonkin's Model of Post-Bereavement Growth proposes that grief does not necessarily shrink over time, rather life grows around it.

FURTHER RESOURCES

Lewis, Dana. 'From Grief to Growth: How I Went from Stuffing My Feelings to Facing Them', *Stop Faking Fine*, https://podcasts.apple.com/gb/podcast/from-grief-to-growth-how-i-went-from-stuffing-my-feelings/id1625569341?i=1000664711206

REFERENCES

Oskis, Andrea. *The Kitchen Shrink*, 2025, Bloomsbury Publishing, p. 241.

Sarner, Moya. 'Why we all need Sisu – the Finnish concept of action and creativity – in hard times', *The Guardian*, 10 February 2025.

Tonkin, L., 2007, cited in Wilson, J. *Supporting People Through Loss and Grief*, 2014, Jessica Kinglsey Publishers, p. 117.

Wilson, Andria. 'The Grief Dance', in *New Techniques of Grief Therapy: Bereavement and Beyond*, edited by Robert Neimeyer, 2022, Routledge, p. 113.

Wilson, Bee. *The Heart-Shaped Tin: Love, Loss and Kitchen Objects*, 2025, Fourth Estate.

For Product Safety Concerns and Information please contact our EU representative GPSR@taylorandfrancis.com
Taylor & Francis Verlag GmbH, Kaufingerstraße 24, 80331 München, Germany

www.ingramcontent.com/pod-product-compliance
Lightning Source LLC
Chambersburg PA
CBHW071822230426
43670CB00013B/2537